FEEDING BABIES & TODDLERS

Jacki Passmore

Photography
Ray Joyce   Mike Hallson

Illustrations
Barbara Rodanska

MURDOCH BOOKS

Sydney • London • Vancouver

THE PUBLISHER THANKS THE
FOLLOWING FOR THEIR
ASSISTANCE

BEECROFT COTTAGE,
BEECROFT

GIFTS PLUS

HANG UPS PRINT GALLERY,
RED HILL

LAURA ASHLEY

ROYAL DOULTON

TEDDY AND FRIENDS

WATERFORD WEDGEWOOD

MRS TONI COLLINS &
MS LINDA DODIMEAD,
DIETITIANS — CHILD AND
FAMILY HEALTH SERVICES

CONTENTS

Breast or Bottle?

Which to choose? It's an important question. These first weeks are the bonding time between mother and child. We show you how to relax and enjoy them together. Your decision is the right one.

BREAST FEEDING IS THE natural choice for the care of your precious new child and is what most mothers choose. It offers the enjoyment of one of life's most intimate experiences, as well as convenience and many long-term benefits for the child.

Every new mother wants to do what is best for her baby, but this must still be fitted in with her own life and its demands. She will be offered lots of advice from well-meaning family and friends, and will receive advice also from the childcare professionals she meets before and after the birth. But in a society where more and more mothers return to the workforce soon after the birth, economics may dictate where the heart and head should perhaps hold sway. The mother who must quickly recommence work, and faces turning care of the new baby over to someone else, may feel cheated out of a very special time. So she should plan to at least begin with breast feeding during her confinement and only change to alternative feeding when necessary. By doing so, both she and baby can enjoy the countless benefits of breast feeding.

Nature's own Vital Contribution

The nursing mother has a vital asset to offer her newborn. It's a transparent, yellowish substance called colostrum. This fluid is in the first secretion from her breasts following the birth, and it is rich in protein, and has less sugar and fat than the breast milk that follows.

In the first three days after the birth, her milk will be composed largely of this fluid. Within six days, its composition will have changed to more closely resemble breast milk, and finally over the next three to four weeks, the milk will assume its normal composition.

Why is colostrum so important? Colostrum is rich in the antibodies that will help build the baby's immunity to many diseases. These same antibodies do not occur in formula preparations. The health of this tiny dependent being, with its immature digestive system and cell structure, needs the extra insurance a nursing mother can offer with these first breast feeds. So even the mother whose circumstances dictate the need to bottle feed should plan to offer the breast for as long as she can. Your nursing advisor will be happy to explain the findings of long research into the benefits of breast feeding.

Successful Breast Feeding

Successful breast feeding should be possible for most mothers, and there is an increasing trend around the world for mothers to choose breast feeding in preference to the bottle feeding favoured a decade or so ago.

We can offer here only basic points towards successful breast and bottle feeding, and urge you to obtain at least one of the specialist publications on early child care recommended by your infant welfare professional, for more detailed discussion of the subject.

Breast feeding has conveniences and joys of a different nature to those experienced by the mother who plans to bottle feed, as we will cover in the following paragraphs. It is easier to fit into a demand-feeding programme, should that be your choice for your baby. Travel and day-to-day activities are not hampered by the equipment needed by the bottle feeding mother. Breast feeding is altogether simpler and safe. It may indeed present momentary embarrassments (usually feared only by the very new mother), such

as when feeding time arrives in a very public place. But such moments are fleeting shadows on an otherwise precious and memorable time for the mother.

Tending the newborn baby should be a joyous experience, but the new mother is often worried about it — usually unnecessarily. The bond between mother and baby is unique and it would be a pity to let inexperience or fear spoil it for you. The mother's concern about inadequate milk supply, nipple problems and feeding difficulties can at times be very and painfully real. There are, however, few problems that cannot be dealt with. A relaxed approach is important, as is good health, and a sensible diet both before and after delivery. Pre-birth preparation and continuing care of the nipples will help prevent painful cracking and other discomforts. Often more helpful perhaps to the new mother is a sympathetic ear. And this is where a patient and understanding partner and family should be ready with helpful reassurance, backed up by a nursing professional.

Your own doctor and support groups, such as nursing mothers' associations, clinics and infant welfare centres are readily accessible, and there is an expanding service in private clinics run by professionals qualified in infant feeding and nursing. These government-sponsored and private professional organisations offer a service available to all mothers, to answer your questions and to offer advice or personal aid.

If you feel the need to talk to other mothers who share your problems and fears, your infant welfare nurse or local clinic should be able to put you in touch with a nursing mothers' association or other such group in your area. These organisations' functions include the distribution of booklets and newsletters, telephone and correspondence counselling and arranging of discussion groups, and they will bring you into contact with other mothers so you can build your own support group. Becoming a mother should mean gaining new friends and acquaintances, rather than a loss of old ones.

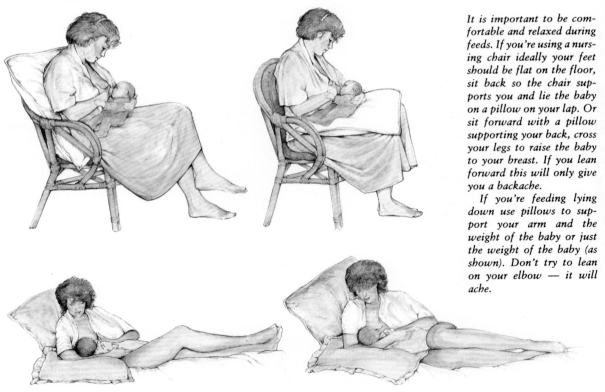

It is important to be comfortable and relaxed during feeds. If you're using a nursing chair ideally your feet should be flat on the floor, sit back so the chair supports you and lie the baby on a pillow on your lap. Or sit forward with a pillow supporting your back, cross your legs to raise the baby to your breast. If you lean forward this will only give you a backache.

If you're feeding lying down use pillows to support your arm and the weight of the baby or just the weight of the baby (as shown). Don't try to lean on your elbow — it will ache.

How and When to Feed

Either before or immediately after the birth, you will be advised on feeding requirements, and a programme will be drawn up for your baby's requirements for its particular weight.

You can at this time also discuss with your nursing advisor what sort of feeding programme to undertake. Some mothers believe that regimented regular feeding will be the best approach, while others choose feeding on demand. There are pros and cons for either method, and the choice should rest with the mother — after all it is she who has to fit the baby's feeding in with her other domestic or work commitments. Rigidity is not always the best path, as we are, after all, dealing with the lives of two individuals — however small one may still be — as well as peripheral people and circumstances.

Successful feeding is enhanced by a quiet, ordered atmosphere in the home. Keep distractions to a minimum so that baby can concentrate on feeding and enjoy the comfort of close contact with the mother. The ease of breast feeding is an obvious advantage, as feeding can be commenced without the delays and inconvenience bottle preparation and heating demand. Consider the joys of remaining in a warm bedroom in the middle of a cold night instead of having to make the trek to a cold kitchen before feeding can begin!

Nipple cleanliness and care should be observed, particularly when the baby is very young. If prenatal instruction has not already covered the topic, you should receive advice in the hospital about this. A few minutes spent each day should ensure comfort and lack of trouble throughout the time you breast feed.

Too often a new mother experiences feeding difficulties simply because the attachment of the baby's mouth to the nipple is not correct. Several factors intervene here. The mild panic experienced by many a new mother as she strives to adjust to this overwhelmingly important new role causes tensions that can manifest themselves in a certain anxiety, or excessive caution in her handling of the child.

A sensible diet and plenty of rest for the mother should ensure adequate milk supply, and most fears usually evaporate as she settles into a feeding routine. The size and shape of the mothers' breasts and nipples are relevant, as is the position in which the baby is held to the breast. Hold baby in such a way that it can enjoy a comfortable, straight-on contact with the nipple, with no obstruction of the nose nor an unnatural angle of the head. Ensure that the baby is warm, without being too snuggly wrapped, and that its body is sufficiently supported to allow it to relax and enjoy its feeding. Maternity staff are there to help you with your first few feedings and after your return home, you can contact your own nursing professional for further advice.

Nipples vary in their sensitivity. Some suggestions to avoid soreness and discomfort are shown here.

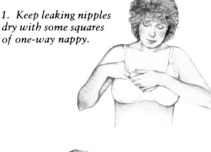

1. Keep leaking nipples dry with some squares of one-way nappy.

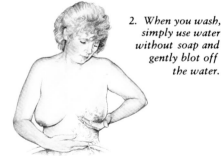

2. When you wash, simply use water without soap and gently blot off the water.

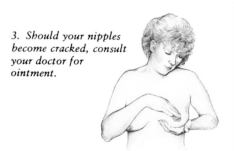

3. Should your nipples become cracked, consult your doctor for ointment.

Some colic and evening irritability are a normal part of the first few months. Breast problems may occur during nursing. Advice from your infant welfare nurse will help solve these promptly, and they don't usually effect the feeding pattern.

When baby is being breast fed there is no requirement for additional vitamin supplements: Nor are water or fruit juices. Breast milk contains all the necessary nutrients for the first six months or so.

The breast-feeding mother's diet is important. Follow guidelines about a balanced diet that contains enough energy or kilojoules and other nutrients. The feeding mother needs to eat more each day than she did before and during the pregnancy, especially around the third month after birth, when the baby is drinking much more.

The mother's diet also affects what is in the breast milk. Alcohol (even one glass of wine) can modify the baby's behaviour because of alcohol tainting the milk. Mothers who are not eating enough of a balanced diet will still make nutritionally adequate breast milk. At dietary extremes, as in the case of Vegan mothers who consume no animal protein (no milk, meat or eggs), the deficiency of vitamin B12 can seriously affect the baby. Medications can also get into breast milk. Not all medications are unsafe, but your doctor should double check before prescribing essential medication.

Plans do not always work out and breast feeding isn't always possible for health or social reasons, and some mothers just do not like the thought of feeding their babies in this way. Babies in this position are lucky that there are now a wide range of both regular and special formulas to suit most needs.

Some nursing mothers do not have enough milk to satisfy their babies' needs, or they wish to work and are unable to breast feed all day and are unable to express enough milk to satisfy their babies in their absence. Then it is all right to combine breast and bottle feeds. It is very important, however, to allow time to find a formula that agrees with the baby before weaning from the breast, especially where allergies may be a problem.

Many of the commercial infant formulas are almost identical in composition, and the choice of one brand over another cannot be made on the basis of superior quality. Sometimes formulas based on cow milk protein cause problems that are not always true allergies or lactose intolerance, and soy-protein-based formulas are better tolerated. Discuss with your family doctor, dietitian, or the sister at your Early Childhood Health Centre what is the best milk formula for your baby.

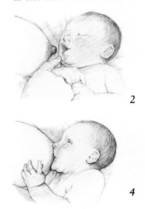
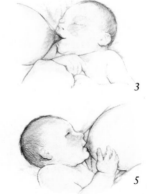

1. When ready to breast feed, prepare the baby to take it by gently stroking the cheek nearest to you.

2. She will turn towards the breast. After a few days the touch of your bare breast against her cheek will be enough for the child to respond.

3. As she turns toward the breast her lips will purse. If brushed with the nipple now . . .

4. . . . she will take to the breast and begin to suck.

5. If she takes only the nipple into her mouth she will get no milk. Her suction and movement of her lips will close the openings.

6. If she uses her jaws to press rhythmically around the base of the areola, while sucking the milk will flow from the nipples. Help her to take the nipple and areola right into her mouth.

Feeding Baby by Bottle

The mother who opts for the bottle feeding knows that she and her child can still enjoy many hours of close contact during feeding and the many other aspects of child care. Feeding your baby from a bottle is more time-consuming in preparation and giving, and of course more costly than breast feeding. But bottle feeding is a necessary option for many mothers and it is important that feelings of guilt do not intrude on the time the mother does spend with the baby.

A number of important points should be considered when bottle feeding. To begin with, cow's milk, whether fresh, powdered or evaporated, is unsuitable for babies younger than ten to twelve months (preferably not younger than 12 months). A wide range of regular and special infant formulas to suit most needs are now available. Discuss with your family doctor, dietitian or your infant welfare nurse the best procedure for your baby and the most suitable formula. Vitamin supplements are usually not required by formula-fed babies, so only give them under the advice of a professional. It may be necessary to offer water during hot or dry conditions, and again this should be at the advice of your infant welfare nurse.

All infant formulas should be made up according to the instructions on the container. Many new mothers need help to get this right and should get one-to-one instruction from their infant welfare nurse on how to do this correctly. A young baby can get very sick if the formula is too strong and, if it is diluted, then the baby may not get enough to eat.

Babies who are breast fed or infant formula fed do not need to have juice or vitamin supplements (syrups/drinks). Breast milk contains vitamin C and all regular infant feeding formulas have added vitamins, including vitamin C.

Sterlising

Bottles must be sterilised for the first 12 months. This can be done by boiling or by submerging them in a sterilising solution. Always wash your hands thoroughly before sterilising the bottles. Rinse the bottles immediately after use and use a bottle brush to clean them thoroughly before sterilising. Make sure the hole in the teat is not clogged with dried milk or formula.

Many interesting commercial juices are available for babies, but it is better to avoid the juice habit. All fruit juices contain significant amounts of sugars which, when given to a baby, can contribute to a) development of a preference for sweet tastes, b) tooth decay and c) loss of appetite for other, necessary foods. They are inappropriate for babies.

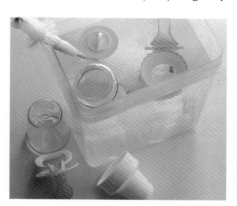

1. Rinse bottles and teats thoroughly in cold water.

2. Use a bottle brush to clean the bottles inside and out.

- Boiling method. Use a large saucepan. Add cold water and the utensils, pushing them under the water and holding them submerged by placing a lid on top. Bring to the boil and boil for 10 minutes. Add the teats in the last 2–3 minutes. When done, leave the bottles in the water until needed.
- Solution sterilising method. The sterilising solution should be used according to the manufacturers' directions. Place the utensils in the solution, weight them to ensure they are submerged and there are no air bubbles, and sterilise for at least one hour. Leave bottles and teats in the solution until needed. Make up a fresh solution each day, and, if you like, rinse bottles before use in boiled water.

Bottles can be made up (24 hours) in advance, and the filled bottles, with teats covered, kept in the refrigerator. Prepared bottles should never be kept at room temperature. Boiled water should always be used, and it should be cooled before mixing. Do not make up formula with boiling water and allow it to cool once made.

Bottles can be warmed by standing them in a jug of hot water. Despite their obvious convenience, the use of microwave ovens for heating babies bottles is discouraged because milk may be unevenly heated, and could scald your baby.

It is just as important in bottle feeding, as in breast feeding that your baby enjoys the warmth of close contact with its mother. Before you begin, ensure your own comfort by sitting in a comfortable chair. Have the formula heated and test it carefully before offering it to baby; your infant welfare nurse will demonstrate the procedure if you are unsure of it. A standard test is to drip a few drops onto the sensitive area of the inside of your wrist. Check that the flow from the teat is neither too fast nor too slow, the former may cause baby to choke, the latter will be such hard work that baby may not take the full amount. The milk should drip, not flow, from the teat.

When they are very young or recently introduced to bottle feeding, babies will need encouragement to feel comfortable with this different feeding technique. Stroke the cheek nearest you, and when baby turns towards your finger, gently press the teat into the mouth. If after several feeds the baby has not settled to a comfortable routine, it may be necessary to use a different style of teat. There are a number of differently shaped ones on the market and amongst those will be a style to suit your baby.

While baby feeds, tilt the bottle so that the teat is full of milk and baby is not sucking in air. Human contact is important to baby's development, so don't rush feeding and don't ignore baby during this time. You may enjoy a few moments in front of television or with a magazine while your baby is feeding, but check frequently that the feed is

3. *Sterilising in a cold water sterilising agent: completely immerse the bottles and teats in solution.*

4. *Sterilising in saucepan or boiler: add teats after water has boiled. Drain bottles thoroughly.*

Your local information centre will probably be able to put you in touch with a nursing mothers' association, which can provide advice, moral support and practical help for breast-feeding mothers.

proceeding smoothly and that your attention has not wandered to the extent that you are holding the bottle at an uncomfortable and unsatisfactory angle. Baby may like the chance to bring up wind half way through feeding, and by doing so can best enjoy the whole feed.

Always throw away any remaining formula or milk, and rinse the bottle and teat thoroughly. Resist the temptation to keep an unfinished bottle for later, as bacteria multiply quickly in warm formula or milk.

Provided the baby is well, comfortable, dry and without wind or allergic reactions to bottle milk or formula, and the choice of a teat is the right one, bottle feeding should not present any major difficulties for either mother or baby.

Weaning Baby

For the nursing mother weaning can bring on a sense of personal loss, as that vital intimate contact is brought to an end. Close and happy mothering at this time makes the adjustment easier for both.

When weaning begins will depend on your own circumstances. It may be necessary within weeks of the birth, or you may choose to breast feed until your baby loses interest in the breast.

For the first six months of life, breast milk contains all the nourishment a baby needs. Around four and a half to six months of age most babies are ready to begin learning to eat different foods, and they may begin with tiny amounts of baby cereal moistened with expressed mother's milk or formula. This introduces baby to new tastes and textures, as well as stimulating the development of chewing.

Whenever you decide to begin weaning, make it a gradual process, to give both yourself and your baby time to adjust to the change. If, for any number of reasons, weaning must take place quickly, consult your infant welfare nurse or another nursing professional on the correct procedures for introducing baby to a new feeding routine, and for the successful drying up of your own milk supply.

If weaning begins at around six months, you may want to make the choice between a cup or a bottle. But do be aware of your baby's stage of development: some are not ready for the new discipline of drinking rather than sucking, and are disturbed by the change. There are many inventive styles of spout fitted to baby cups which may be useful. Your baby may prefer to go onto and stay on a bottle for many months to come. But do start to encourage drinking from a cup at around 7–8 months.

If baby is not yet being breast fed, a proprietary infant formula is strongly recommended until he reaches twelve months, after which he can be switched to cow's milk. No vitamin supplements are required with formula feeding, provided you use a recommended brand. A suitable multi-vitamin supplement is usually recommended until at least the end of the first year for babies having cow's milk instead of formula or breast.

When breast feeding, if any problems develop, such as sore or cracked nipples, always seek medical advice promptly. An antibiotic cream will usually solve the problem very quickly.

Milk Allergy and Intolerance

Often a child who is allergic to a protein in his diet may display some seemingly unrelated symptoms, such as eczema or asthma. When the symptoms are clearly digestive, such as diarrhoea, it may be difficult to be sure if the problem is an allergy or a kind of food or drink intolerance, and often they are interrelated.

Should your baby prove to be intolerant to a cow's milk formula, seek the advice of your infant welfare nurse on the use of substitute milks, such as soy milk. There may not always be a simple solution to a problem. Some children may be allergic to both cow's milk and soy bean milk. It is important not to leap to conclusions but to seek medical advice with an open mind.

Remember that at this early stage of life the milk your baby drinks should provide all his nutritional needs.

Skim milk, fat-reduced or other treated milks will NOT provide adequate nourishment for your baby and should NEVER be given except on the advice of a doctor.

Dairy products, such as yoghurt and cheese, should not be given to a baby in place of milk until at least nine months of age. If baby enjoys them, you may consider partial replacement of milk at nine months. 1 cup of natural yoghurt is the equivalent of 1 cup of milk, or 30 grams (1 oz) cheese of the firm cheddar variety. (See Feeding Problems and Allergies page 50.)

Mixed Feeding

How, when and why you introduce solids into baby's diet. Babies are individuals with differing needs, so there can be no hard and fast rules about this important step. Our basic guidelines on timing, quantities and food suggestions, plus different ways to prepare and cook your own baby foods, should help you through this stage.

Rice Cereal, Toast Fingers with Vegemite, and Juice

For the proud mother boasting that her two-month-old is already eating solids, it's a hollow victory.

There are no sound medical or nutritional reasons for a baby to be fed anything but breast milk or formula for the first six months of life. In fact, in her eagerness for the child to progress, this mother could be doing her child a serious disservice. The infant digestive tract is not fully developed. Upsets, severe pain and even more serious consequences can result from the too-early introduction of solid foods.

Additionally, the baby's immunity to disease-causing bacteria is low, particularly in the case of the formula-fed baby. Bacteria can be introduced easily through the use of unsterile food utensils, cooking equipment and the food itself.

Wanting your child to be the best is a natural parental instinct, but child rearing is not a competition. Your child's interests and well-being must always be your prime goal, and her diet should reflect your concern.

Milk is a Whole Food

Milk alone provides sufficient nourishment for the baby up to the sixth month. Babies who are no longer breast fed should be given a regular infant formula as a drink until one year of age. For babies with no special needs, the milk intake after the age of 7 months varies between 700 and 1000 mL each day. The quantities of mixed feeds (containing meat, vegetables, cereals, fruits) may need to be increased if the baby does not seem to be satisfied. Babies who are drinking more than a litre of milk a day, to the exclusion of other foods, may be missing out on other essential nutrients like iron.

Why rush the introduction of mixed feeding? Why give yourself the extra work of preparing baby foods when it's neither necessary nor desirable? Your baby's eating habits will not necessarily mature faster from an earlier beginning.

That First Spoonful

When you feel that it is time for mixed feeding to begin, usually around the fifth or sixth month, your baby may be growing quickly and be happy to receive the extra nourishment. But many babies still do not, at this stage, require more than milk alone. It will be a time of experimentation, and if after several attempts your baby is still not interested, delay it for another few weeks. Babies reach a stage when they require the extra nourishment in their own time, and they are usually quick to let their mothers know about it. Obvious signs are fretfulness after feeding or gnawing of fists.

If there is unwillingness to eat, remember that the action of swallowing has up to this time only been associated with sucking. Your baby may cough, splutter and spit the food straight back out. Patience and gentle persistence will help her to gradually understand the idea of swallowing food.

Rice Cereal First

A rice cereal is the best choice of first food, as it is easiest to digest. Choose a commercially prepared dry cereal to be diluted with breast milk, water or formula, or make your own with whole grain polished, powdered or ground rice. Wheat contains gluten, to which some people are highly allergic. Avoid wheat-based cereals until baby is at least seven months old. Commercial baby cereals have the advantages of being pre-cooked and iron-fortified.

The quantity will be minute. Little more than a half teaspoon at first, diluted to the consistency of cream. The mixture should not be liquid. The principal aim of this feeding exercise is to introduce solids and to train your baby to swallow. You may find that she has more success with a thicker consistency. Experiment, and settle on whatever best suits.

The nursing mother will see the wisdom of using expressed breast milk to dilute the cereal for these initial feeds. Its familiar taste and smell will help the baby to relate to the new food. After several days, formula or water can be added. Try mixing it with orange juice occasionally. Your child may enjoy the novel taste.

When you first introduce solids, even very mushy foods, you may find less resistance if you use a very small spoon and only half-fill it. It can be quite scary for a baby if a huge, shiny, overloaded spoon comes flying through the air towards their relatively small mouth. There is also less to wipe off the floor, should the offering prove unacceptable.

What Time is Best?

For the first year baby's meal times are unlikely to coincide with your own. First meals require concentration and harmony. Choose a time when the household is in order and there will be no disturbances.

An immature digestive system is probably best able to cope with solid foods at the mid-morning feed. Morning hunger will have been satisfied by the early morning bottle or breast feed, but by now the baby has been active and building up an appetite for several hours.

It makes sense to offer the first taste of this different food at the hungriest time — before mid-morning milk — assuming that she will be more receptive. If she is really hungry, the baby is unlikely to accept a new, unfamiliar food, and will probably not co-operate.

Taking the edge off her hunger by offering half of the normal feed is possibly the most satisfactory approach. Then you can take your time with the cereal, and finish with the reassuringly familiar breast or bottle. However many mothers find that in the very early stages of introducing solids, they get the best results by offering just a small amount of solids before feeding. Try both ways and see which best suits your child.

Keep in mind that these feeds will be slow and messy. The baby is more likely to dribble the food straight back out than to swallow it. The process of feeding just a small teaspoonful can take some minutes. It should not be forced.

Offering solid foods at the end of a normal feed will be pointless, unless your child has already developed a strong requirement for additional nourishment.

Don't Offer New Foods at Night

The new mother appreciates any tactic which promises an unbroken night's sleep. Therefore many are inclined to offer solids with the late night 10 pm feed, on the assumption that baby will sleep soundly on a full tummy. This does work with some children, but for others a full stomach at night can cause painful colic and you'll both be in for a bad night.

Preparation and Warming

Babies do not appear to be bothered by cold food. It is adults who have been

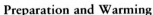

Chicken, Egg and Carrot Custard (page 26)

Cottage cheese and Apple (page 25), steamed carrots, sweet potato and potato sticks

conditioned to appreciate hot food. If it pleases you, warm the cereal or the milk used to dilute it. Never make it too warm: what may seem tepid to you could be hot to your baby.

• Always wash your hands thoroughly before feeding.

• Place the dish of prepared food over a cup or jug of boiling water just until it no longer feels cold.

• Ensure that the dish and spoon you're using have been thoroughly washed and rinsed first. Drip-dry utensils for baby rather than wipe with a cloth.

• Use only thoroughly cleaned pans and metal (not wooden) spoons for cooking.

• Prepare only as much as is needed if using dry cereals. If cooking your own, prepare small quantities and store the remainder in the refrigerator for no more than one day. Don't leave cooked rice at room temperature for any length of time, or cook more than you will use that day, as bacteria develop in this type of cereal.

• Do not save uneaten portions of food offered to the baby. Saliva will have been introduced to the food and the bacteria will multiply quickly.

Successful First Feeding

This comes from having the right equipment. A baby cannot be expected to enjoy spoon feeding if it's done with a rough edged spoon that's too big. A coffee spoon is suitable, though a small-sized plastic baby feeding spoon will be better, as plastic does not transmit heat or cold.

• Sit the baby comfortably on your lap or in a baby chair.

• Tie a bib in place and hold the baby's head gently but firmly so that a sudden turn does not result in an eye or ear full.

• Place the spoon in her mouth on top of the tongue. Remove it with an upwards motion so the food is pushed off by the top gum or lip.

• Offer no more than a few drops at a time at first. And if she spits it straight back, gently retrieve it from her chin and return it to her mouth. Gradually she will begin to swallow.

If she is unwilling to eat after a few attempts, discard the food and begin again later with a new preparation. If she finds it difficult to move a spoonful of food

from the front to the back of the mouth, and seems to be spitting the food out, it may be necessary to give solids and not liquids, the food needs to be placed in the centre of the tongue.

The baby may cough and sneeze at first. Hold a hand or a cloth in front of her face, not over her mouth. A hand is much easier to wash than the kitchen floor. Once she's accustomed to the concept of swallowing, she'll soon begin chewing.

When eating reflexes are at work, it won't be long before the baby is enjoying coarser textures in food. Gradually increase the daily consumption to about four teaspoons by the end of the fifth month.

• Never attempt to feed your baby cereals from a bottle using a teat with an enlarged hole. Cereals are intended as a supplement to the normal intake of milk. Your baby does not have to consume a great quantity of solid food yet. If she will not take it from a spoon, simply try again later.

• Expect a mess, and some show of resistance from your child. Deal with these problems without signs of distress to maintain the trust you've established through your milk feeding.

• Baby's bowel movements should change once solid foods are introduced. They may be flecked with undigested food, which should not be a concern. If there is evidence of diarrhoea, you may be giving too much food or there may be a reaction to it. Remove it from the diet until the condition stabilises. Consult your doctor if the symptoms continue.

New Tastes

Your baby will enjoy and should be able to tolerate several different foods in the early weeks of spoon feeding.

Nature's own convenience food, the banana, is one of the best. Choose well-ripened fruits as they are easier to digest. Mash with a fork and serve straight, mixed with cereal or a little orange juice.

Apple cooked and thoroughly mashed, can be served with cereal, mashed banana or orange juice, or on its own. Gradually increase the thickness and texture as your baby learns to chew.

Some children of only four to five months enjoy chewing. Infant gums can be just as good as teeth. Be selective with

Always burp a baby after feeding. There are various methods, but you do need to spend at least 10 minutes to get the wind up properly. Vague patting does nothing but annoy the baby and exhaust you — baby's stomach needs to be kept flat, usually against your shoulder, while you gently but fairly firmly rub the back in a circular motion, trying to massage excess air out of the stomach. This eases indigestion and helps the baby to settle.

Your local baby health centre can give you the most up-to-date expert advice.

Try to relax about the whole question of feeding. A new parent, alone in the house with a first baby and no one to talk to, can sometimes get things out of proportion and start worrying quite unnecessarily if the baby rejects a feed or a particular solid food for a day or two. Try something else, ring a friend, have a chat and relax. No baby deliberately starves itself to death.

finger foods at this age. Give very firm foods only, such as a rusk or hard crust. Not only is the danger of choking ever-present, but foods such as raw apple or carrot are difficult for the child to digest.

Food Intolerance

Fretful crying, spots and rashes, vomiting and diarrhoea are indicators that all is not well. Seek advice from your infant welfare nurse. If the symptoms begin immediately after or within a short time of the introduction of a new food this may indicate food intolerance. Remove the new food from the baby's diet. You may try the food again, in moderation, at a later date.

Do not become your own medical adviser. Consult your doctor.

How Much Solid Food?

The individual requirement for solid foods will vary. A good rule is to watch your child's rate of bottle consumption, or note diminishing interest in breast feeding.

Leaving some formula in the bottle, or cutting feeding time short may mean that she is being satisfied by solids. Remember, for the first year milk is the most important food for your baby. Adjust her intake of solids until she resumes her normal milk consumption.

If the bottle is finished quickly, or the baby seems fretful after nursing, try gradually increasing the amount of solid foods, not the amount of milk. Constant fretfulness is a sign that all is not well. Seek advice from your infant welfare nurse.

Establishing a Feeding Program

How often the young baby receives his first solid meals each day will depend largely on individual needs.

Within two months of the introduction of solid foods, your child's consumption may have increased to as much as six or eight tablespoons of solids daily, including a number of different foods. By this time baby may be enjoying three meals a day.

Here is a simple schedule which will be helpful as baby begins to take his first solids. New foods should not be introduced too quickly.

First to second week:
Mid-morning: 1–2 teaspoons iron-fortified baby cereal, mixed with expressed breast milk, formula or cooled, boiled water.

Second to third week:
Mid-morning: 1–2 teaspoons thoroughly mashed, cooked fruit or vegetable.
Mid-afternoon 3–4 teaspoons cereal, prepared as above.

After third week:
Mid-morning: Up to 2 tablespoons fruit or vegetable, prepared as above.
Mid-afternoon: Up to 2 tablespoons cereal, prepared as above.

Variety in the diet is not yet important. Your baby would probably be content with the same foods at each meal. You can start selecting new foods to interest her, however. Some will be accepted with relish, others rejected without a taste. Offer them again in a few weeks time. First impressions are not always lasting ones.

At least one of your baby's mealtimes may now coincide with a family meal, though it is too early yet to begin to establish the ground rules for table and mealtime etiquette.

Eggs

Although eggs are a convenient and nourishing, it is important that they are not introduced too early. Recent studies have found high bacteria counts in some eggs tested, and egg whites have also been known to cause allergic reaction, especially if there is a family history of allergy.

Begin to introduce egg into your baby's diet in the seventh month. Hard-boiled eggs are, perhaps surprisingly, more easily digested than soft-cooked. Serve only the yolk first, giving no more than ¼ teaspoon at each feed. Increase this gradually until the whole yolk is taken. You can serve it plain or mashed with a little milk or formula. It's great also with mashed banana, yoghurt or avocado.

Never give the young child raw or even lightly cooked eggs. These can be contaminated with a micro-organism which can cause serious stomach upsets, even food poisoning. Wait for several weeks after giving egg yolks before offering the whites, then gradually increase the quantity and watch for signs of reaction.

If your child enjoys eggs and experiences no reaction, you can use eggs in a wide variety of easy-to-prepare baby meals.

Finger Foods

As your child's hand-eye co-ordination matures, one of her first achievements will be to bring things to her mouth. By six to eight months the child will enjoy first attempts at feeding herself.

Finger foods are to nibble on, suck, paint with, throw and squish. Do not discourage your baby from enjoying these pursuits, despite the mess. The more practice she gets in feeding herself at this elementary stage, the sooner she'll be reaching into the plate with a spoon. Independence is natural and desirable.

Ideal Finger Foods for the 6–8 month-old

Table water biscuits: light, crisp texture which pulps easily, low sugar.
Rusks: make for gnawing on and great during teething.
Toast fingers: save breakfast leftovers.
Soft crusts: little chewy bits can be mashed off with determined gums.
Sticks of cooked carrot, potato, pumpkin, sweet potato: cooked, not raw at this age.
A smooth chop bone: leave tiny scrapings of meat attached.
Arrowroot biscuits: the all-time favourite.
A peeled banana: it's messy, but it's nice.

A Word of Caution

There is one obvious danger in the use of finger foods. Mother will be tempted to slip away for a few quiet moments by herself, or get a few important chores done while baby is content with the new treat. *Don't.* One small piece of food gnawed off the end of a bread finger can wedge in the throat. A sliver of cracker can be sucked into an air passage, or a chop bone could be poked into an eye.

Choking

It is normal for babies to gag on new foods. However, if choking occurs the following course of action is recommended.

If the child is coughing and not turning blue in the face there is not much need to worry as the child is receiving air, and will possibly 'cough up' the food himself.

If, however, the child is gasping for air, panicking that he cannot breath and turning scarlet or grey in the face then you may need to perform the 'Heimlich manoeuvre'. Get your doctor to show you the technique. To do this, lie the child face up on your lap or on a flat surface. Place your fingers (the pads of the middle and index fingers) on the child's abdomen, slightly above the navel and well below the rib cage. Gently press in upward thrusts into the abdomen to dislodge the obstruction.

Vegetable Omelette (page 26)

Safety

Always supervise a child when eating. Small, hard foods can be easily inhaled and are therefore dangerous. Do not offer hard lollies, popcorn, raw carrot or apple, peas and sweet corn. Nuts (whole or chopped) are generally offered after 7 years of age. Leafy vegetables are often fibrous and hard to swallow.

Also avoid sweet foods including chocolate (what babies don't know about they can't begin to crave); fresh bread, which can stick to the roof of the mouth, is difficult for a baby to eat.

Teething

Steamed Minced Veal on Spinach (page 30) and Junket (page 30) with yoghurt

Teething can be a trying time for both mother and child. Baby will need to gnaw on things to relieve the discomfort of the gums. Many favourite finger foods are useful at this time. Offer rusks, a smooth, cooked cutlet bone, fingers of thick bread dried to firm in a warm oven, or a chilled teething ring. Baby may be fretful during feeding times and biting may cause discomfort for the breast-feeding mother. Some nursing mothers find that, at this time, it helps to break feeds up into several short sessions, so baby feeds properly rather than chews. When teeth first appear, start gently, cleaning your child's teeth with a child's toothbrush or soft cloth. Seek professional advice on the application of anaesthetic gum preparations before use. Do not give aspirin.

Pacifiers

To use a pacifier or not will be another of those choices the mother must make herself. It is now widely accepted that sucking a dummy, thumb or fingers is unlikely to affect the natural growth and shape of the teeth and gums, and it can be an enormous comfort to a child.

It is unwise, to tempt a child with a pacifier that has been sweetened. Undiluted juices, honey and glycerine are the main culprits, and the result of continual gum contact with these strong sweeteners can be harmful. The teeth can begin to decay as soon as they erupt, and may be lost at a very early age. The loss of milk teeth can affect the subsequent development of the gums and jawline, affecting the child's ability to chew.

Baby's First Meals

For the six to ten-month-olds:

Cereals: including breakfast cereals, pasta, bread, rice, protein rich, oatmeal, barley, wheat

Vegetables: avocado, beans, broccoli, carrots, dried beans and peas, pumpkin, spinach, squash, sweet potato (yam)

Fruit: apples, apricots, bananas, nectarines, pears, peaches, plums, prunes, pineapple

Juice: orange, apple, grape, blackcurrant (unsweetened and well diluted)

Eggs: yolks and whole, after seven months

Cow's milk: introduce slowly in cereal

from ten to twelve months and watch for reactions. It should be boiled. Do not give fat-reduced or skim milk. Consult a professional before giving soybean milk.

Meat: chicken, lamb, livers, fish. Fat-free broth is easily digested and nutritious.

Cheese: Cheddar type cheeses, creamed cottage cheese, ricotta, yoghurt, butter. Do not substitute dairy products for milk until after nine months.

Suggested meals to be used only when each food has been individually introduced

Breakfasts:
> Cereal, cereal with fruit, cereal with creamed cottage cheese
> Hard-boiled egg yolk mashed with milk or cheese
> Scrambled egg
> Mashed banana with rice or barley cereal or creamed cottage cheese
> Mashed banana or apple with fruit juice
> Mashed apple
> Mashed avocado with sieved hard-boiled egg yolk

Lunches:
> Puréed liver and vegetables
> Puréed chicken and livers with vegetables
> Mashed vegetables with egg yolk
> Lentil and vegetables
> Mashed avocado with creamed cottage cheese
> Banana pudding

Dinners:
> Creamed cottage cheese with mashed fruit or vegetables
> Vegetable omelette
> Chicken, egg and carrot custard
> Mashed sweet potato (yam) and apple
> Rice cream
> Egg yolk custard

Foods should be cooked without salt or sugar. Offer the foods separately so baby can learn to distinguish individual tastes and textures. At first foods should be thoroughly mashed. By about the seventh month, foods should be fork mashed or finely chopped to encourage proper chewing habits.

The recipes for these meals and for frozen baby foods follow.

Rice or Barley Cereal

Wash 1 cup (185 g) of short grain polished rice or barley thoroughly and drain. Pour the rice into a saucepan and add 5 cups (1.25 L) of water. Bring to the boil, boil for 1–2 minutes, then cover tightly and reduce the heat to very low. Simmer gently until the liquid has been absorbed and the cereal is a thick soft paste. Pour into ice cube trays and freeze.

Ground Rice Cereal

Grind ¼ cup (75 g) of short grain polished rice to a smooth powder in a food processor or blender. Transfer to the top of a double saucepan and add 1 cup (250 mL) of milk, or half milk and half water. Stir until it begins to boil, then cook gently, stirring occasionally until thick and creamy (about 12 minutes).

Oat Porridge

Grind ¼ cup (25 g) of rolled oats to a fine powder in a food processor or blender. Cook in the top of a double saucepan with ¼ cup (60 mL) of water and ¾ cup (185 mL) of milk until smooth and creamy, about 12 minutes.

Apple

Peel and slice apples and remove the cores. In an enamel or stainless steel saucepan simmer the fruit in water until tender — for 1 cup (185 g) of fruit use ¼ cup (60 mL) water.

Or grate uncooked fruit, peeled and core, and simmer for 5-6 minutes, again using 1 cup of fruit to ¼ cup (60 mL) of water.

Or bake whole apples wrapped in aluminium foil in a moderate oven 180°C (350°F/Gas 4) until tender, about 35 minutes. Remove the skins and scrape off the flesh with a spoon.

Apple and Sweet Potato

Cut equal amounts of peeled apple and sweet potato into small cubes and place in a dish. Set in a steamer and steam until tender, about 12 minutes, then mash with a little apple juice. Add ricotta cheese to give a creamier texture. Freeze in small quantities. (Offer cheese recipe after nine months.)

> Each new food should be introduced as a teaspoonful at the first feeding. Wait a day before giving more and only introduce new foods every few days until the basics are established.

Vegetables with Egg Yolk

To be used after seven months. Boil or steam 1–2 tablespoons of diced mixed vegetables (peas, broccoli, pumpkin) until tender. Drain and mash. Pass the yolk of a hard-boiled egg through a fine nylon sieve and mix with the vegetables.

Lentil and Vegetables

Boil 1–2 tablespoons of soaked lentils or split peas in water until tender. Drain and mash the peas, then mix with an equal amount of mashed mixed vegetables. Add a little milk or cottage cheese.

Vegetable Omelette

Mix 1 tablespoon of mashed or chopped cooked vegetables with 1 beaten egg and 2 teaspoons of water or milk. Melt 1 teaspoon of butter in a small frying pan or saucepan and pour in the omelette mixture. Cook gently, stirring occasionally, until egg sets.

Chicken, Egg and Carrot Custard

Baked Potato with Egg and Yoghurt (page 28)

Finely grate 1 tablespoon of raw carrot and mince 1–2 tablespoons of uncooked chicken. Mix with 1 beaten egg and 2 teaspoons of water or milk. Pour into 2 small greased dishes or custard cups and cover with aluminium foil. Set in a bain marie* and bake in a moderate oven 180°C (350°F/Gas 4) for about 20 minutes.

Liver and Vegetables

In a small tightly closed saucepan poach 60 g of calf's liver in 2 tablespoons of milk, until tender (about 6 minutes). Remove and purée with a little of the milk. Boil or steam 1–2 tablespoons of vegetables (pumpkin, peas, broccoli) and mash to serve with the liver paste.

Chicken and Chicken Livers in Gravy

In a small saucepan poach 45 g of chicken and 45 g of chicken livers in 2 tablespoons of milk and 2 tablespoons of water. Simmer very gently, tightly covered, for about 12 minutes. Remove the meat and purée or blend with a little of the liquid. Return to the remaining liquid and simmer until it forms a thick paste.

Rice Cream

In the top of a double saucepan, simmer 1 tablespoon of powdered rice (polished short grain rice ground in a blender) or rice flour with ¾ cup (185 mL) of milk and simmer, stirring until smooth and creamy.

Egg Yolk Custard

Beat together 1 whole egg and 1 egg yolk and mix with 2 teaspoons of milk. Pour into a small dish or custard cup and steam for about 6 minutes until set.

Banana Pudding

Mash a half banana with ¼ cup (60 mL) milk, ½ teaspoon rice flour and 1 egg yolk. Pour into 2 small greased custard cups or Chinese tea cups and set in a bain marie.* Bake in a moderate oven 180°C (350°F/Gas 4) for about 30 minutes until set. Serve warm or cold. These can be steamed for about 8 minutes, instead of baking.

* *An oven dish containing warm water which comes halfway up the sides of the custard cups.*

More to Choose From

As your child grows she will be ready to accept different tastes and textures. From the tenth month many new foods can be added to the preceding list and from these you'll have a wide scope for preparing flavoursome and nutritious meals. But as the baby may not like some of the seasonings, coarser textures and strong tastes of the dishes we cook for ourselves, you may have to consider alternatives or adjustments to your recipes.

The preparation of baby foods should not be allowed to dominate your kitchen activities. With a little planning and advance preparation, you should be able to cook meals for baby without upsetting your routine.

Plan to cook dishes using the meats, fruits and vegetables you've bought for your own meal. You could cook more plain vegetables and roast or stewed meats than you need. The extra can be incorporated into the baby's next meal.

Keep a supply of frozen food *cubes* or *drops* on hand (pages 32–33).

Improvise on the following recipes so you can use available meat and vegetables. Remember the invaluable egg when you're short on time and ideas.

The following new foods can now be used in your baby's meals. It is wise to take the precaution of introducing new foods in moderation with a two or three day interval between each.

Cereals and Grains: bread, macaroni, noodles, pasta shells, spaghetti

Crackers: water biscuits, unsweetened crackers, crispbread

Fruit: dried fruits (cooked)

Vegetables: asparagus, cauliflower, cabbage, eggplant (aubergine), potatoes, tomatoes

Meat: beef, beef heart and other offal (variety meats), turkey, veal

Fish: any white fish (no shellfish at all)

Dessert ingredients: sago, tapioca, cornflour (corn-starch), gelatine

Yoghurt: plain and unsweetened only

Meal Suggestions

Breakfast:
> Yoghurt with fruit
> Bread/toast with creamed cottage cheese/Vegemite or Marmite
> Bread/toast with scrambled or poached egg

Lunches:
> Yoghurt with fruit salad or vegetables
> Poached fish with mashed potato and peas
> Steamed fish with diced vegetables
> Stewed beef and vegetables
> Noodles with chicken in white sauce
> Cauliflower in creamy sauce
> Baked potato with egg and yoghurt
> Cream soup with toast/bread fingers
> Fruit dessert
> Fruit jelly

Dinners:
> Creamed cottage cheese on crispbread or toast
> Steamed minced veal on spinach
> Poached brains on vegetables
> Home-made baked beans on toast (recipe on page 93)
> Bread omelette
> Vegetable rice custard
> Junket
> Yoghurt jelly

Establish sensible eating patterns now. Do not automatically serve a sweet dish as dessert after a meal, but if you want to serve something extra, offer a small dish of yoghurt and slivers of fresh or canned fruit.

Discourage excessive between-meals snacking. Offer foods which are not high in sugar, salt or fat.

Give plenty of water, baby's full requirement of milk and occasionally offer diluted fruit juice.

The following recipes are suitable for children from ten months.

Scrambled Egg in a Double Saucepan

Lightly beat 1 whole egg and 1 egg yolk with 1 tablespoon of milk. Melt 1 teaspoon of butter in the top of a double saucepan and pour in the egg. Cover and cook over gently boiling water until the egg begins to set underneath. Stir lightly

When feeding your baby solids, a lot of it may end up on the baby. Try not to cover your child's face with a washer or flannel: children tend to panic and scream when they can't see, can't speak and above all, can't breathe. Gently wipe around the mouth a little at a time.

Sometimes when children are teething, they go off their food. Don't panic. Ensure that the child drinks plenty of milk or water. If your child won't take fluids, then consult your doctor, and take the advised steps to prevent dehydration.

and cook until just set. Serve with fingers of buttered bread or soft toast. Scrambled eggs cook well and quickly in the microwave.

Poached Egg

Successful egg poaching can be done without an egg poacher. Bring a medium-sized saucepan of water to the boil and add a teaspoon of lemon juice or vinegar. (This helps to keep the white attached to the yolk.) Stir the water briskly in one direction only. Break a fresh egg into a cup and slide into the centre of the swirling water. The white should immediately wrap itself around the yolk. Simmer until the white is firm and the yolk softly cooked, about 1¼ minutes. Lift out on a slotted spoon.

Use only fresh eggs. Older eggs tend to separate, and the white runs off in strands.

Bread Omelette

This is an easy and inexpensive meal for your child. Soak a quarter slice of wholemeal bread in milk until softened, then squeeze out the milk and break the bread into tiny pieces. Beat 1 egg lightly, mix with the bread and 2 teaspoons of milk. Melt ½ teaspoon of butter in a small frying pan and pour in the egg mixture. Cook gently until lightly coloured on the underside, then turn on the other side until cooked through.

Eggy Potatoes

Beat 1 egg into 2 tablespoons of leftover mashed potato and steam or microwave in a small dish or fry in 1 teaspoon butter until the egg is set.

Baked Potato with Egg and Yoghurt

Boil 1 medium-sized potato, well scrubbed, in its jacket until tender. Slit open and scoop out the centre. Pass half a hard-boiled egg yolk through a nylon sieve and mix with 2 teaspoons of plain yoghurt and the potato, well mashed. Return to the potato case.

Cauliflower in Creamy Sauce

Break about 60 g of fresh or frozen cauliflower into small sprigs and boil or steam until tender. Mix 2 tablespoons milk with

1 teaspoon of dry milk powder or ricotta cheese and ¾ teaspoon cornflour (cornstarch). Stir in a small saucepan until thickened. Drain the cauliflower thoroughly, chop or mash, and stir into the sauce.

Use this recipe also for diced carrots, tiny sprigs of broccoli, diced asparagus or pumpkin.

Poached Fish with Potato and Peas

Place a 60 g piece of white fish in a small saucepan and add milk to cover. Cover the pan and simmer for 3–5 minutes until tender. Boil a small new potato with 1–2 teaspoons of frozen peas until tender. Drain, peel the potato and mash with the peas and a little milk from the fish. Flake the fish and serve with the vegetables.

Steamed Fish and Diced Vegetables

Cut a 60 g piece of white fish into cubes and place in a small dish with 2 tablespoons of finely diced fresh vegetables (carrot, broccoli, asparagus) including some frozen peas. Steam until the vegetables are tender, about 8 minutes. Flake the fish and chop with the vegetables, adding a little milk, or the liquid accumulated in the dish, to give a smooth consistency.

Poached Brains with Vegetables

Soak a set of sheep's brains in cold water for 1 hour, changing the water several times. Remove any skin and membrane and transfer to a saucepan. Cover with fresh cold water and add a few drops of lemon juice. Bring to the boil, then reduce the heat and simmer for 20–25 minutes. Drain. Boil or steam 2 tablespoons of mixed diced vegetables (carrots, peas, broccoli, cauliflower) until tender. Purée the vegetables with 1 teaspoon of ricotta cheese or milk and add the brains, mashing to a smooth paste.

Stewed Beef and Vegetables

In a small saucepan place about 90 g of lean beef steak or veal, 1 new potato, 1 small carrot, and a small pickling onion. Add a small piece of bay leaf and a sprig of parsley, then cover with water. Cover the saucepan, bring to the boil, then simmer gently until the meat is tender. Add

Scrambled Eggs (page 27), Toast Fingers and Bread Omelette (opposite)

more water as needed. Grind or purée the ingredients with a little of the cooking liquid. Discard the bay leaf and parsley.

Steamed Minced Veal on Spinach

Mix 90 g of finely minced veal with 1 beaten egg and 1 teaspoon of cornflour. Place ½ cup (25 g) finely chopped fresh or frozen spinach in a small dish and spread the meat over it. Steam for about 10 minutes or microwave in a covered dish for about 3 minutes.

Use this recipe also for turkey, chicken or kidneys. Serve with a spoonful of white or cream sauce, or simply mix the meat with the spinach.

Vegetable Rice Custard

Mix 1 tablespoon of mixed puréed vegetables with 1 tablespoon of leftover cooked rice and 1 egg yolk. Add ¼ cup (60 mL) of milk and pour into 2 lightly buttered tea cups or custard cups. Cover with aluminium foil and bake in a bain marie in a moderate oven 180°C (350°F/Gas 4) for about 30 minutes.

Noodles with Chicken in White Sauce

Drop 1 tablespoon of crumbled egg noodles into a small saucepan of boiling water to simmer until soft. Drain and set aside. Finely mince 60 g of boneless chicken and place in the saucepan with milk to cover. Simmer gently until tender, then mash with the milk and return to the saucepan. Add 1 teaspoon cornflour mixed with a little cold water and stir until the sauce thickens, then mix in the noodles.

Cream Soup

Boil diced vegetables and/or meat until tender in a mixture of milk and water. Lift out and purée with some of the liquid, then return to the soup and add 1–3 teaspoons of dry milk powder.

Thicken if needed with a mixture of cornflour and cold water.

- For extra richness stir in a lightly beaten egg yolk mixed with the cornflour and water.
- Young children find eating soup difficult. Help them to enjoy it by using a cup.

- Serve soup with crackers, crispbread or butter toast.

Fruit Dessert

Mix 1 cup (250 mL) of unsweetened fruit juice with 1 tablespoon of cornflour in a small saucepan. Boil, stirring, until thickened and clear. Pour into small dishes and refrigerate until cool. Serve with plain yoghurt or fruit.

Fruit Jelly

Sprinkle 1½ tablespoons of unflavoured gelatine over ½ cup (125 mL) of cool water in a small saucepan. Heat through, then add 1½ cups (375 mL) of unsweetened fruit juice and heat through again. Pour into a mixing bowl and leave until beginning to thicken. Stir in ¾ cup of puréed fresh or canned fruit or ¾ (185 mL) of milk and whisk with an electric beater until fluffy. Transfer to small glass dishes and refrigerate until set.

Yoghurt Jelly

Using the above recipe, add 1 cup (250 mL) of plain yoghurt and 1 tablespoon of sugar instead of the puréed fruit or milk. Then refrigerate.

Junket

An all-time favourite with children. Use the unflavoured junket tablets while the baby is still young and make an extra creamy junket by adding milk powder to the milk and just enough brown sugar to lightly sweeten. Follow the instructions on the packet closely. If the milk is not at exactly the right temperature the junket will not set. Serve with fresh or canned puréed fruit.

Vegemite (Marmite) and Cheese Rusks

Spread day-old bread with Vegemite and cover with a thin layer of grated cheese. Cut into fingers and bake in a slow oven 150°C (300°F/Gas 2) for 1½–2 hours until really hard. Store in an airtight container.

Don't encourage your child to drink milk or juice immediately before meals, as it can spoil the appetite. It is much better for the digestive system to not drink at all with meals. Try to wait at least 15 minutes after a meal.

Commercial Baby Foods

Canned, packaged and bottled baby foods are useful for the busy mother, and as a working mother I would be the last person to suggest they be avoided. The range of commercially prepared baby foods available in our supermarkets is very comprehensive. It covers single foods like cereals, fruits, juices, vegetables and meats. There are also desserts, combination dinners and baked goods. Most supermarkets stock one or two well-known brands, and prices generally remain competitive between the brands.

Should we use these prepared foods? Why not? They were designed for convenience, and they are just that. They are not intended to replace every meal — they lack the texture necessary to stimulate chewing skills. They don't help baby learn to discern taste and flavour (smell).

They are bacterially safe. The heating process required for canned and bottled foods and the drying process used for cereals and some baked goods destroys harmful bacteria. Added salt has been almost totally eliminated and the use of MSG (monosodium glutamate) as a flavour enhancer has been discontinued. The foods are no longer chemically preserved, and nutrient loss is minimal. The foods are cooked, then immediately canned or bottled, sealed and cooled, with most of the goodness being locked in. Often extra vitamins and minerals have been added and some have additional protein in the form of soya or other vegetable proteins.

Yet there are additives, in the form of stabilisers, fillers, flavour enhancers, anti-caking agents and others. These may be safe in themselves, but could not be considered an essential part of a good diet. Some products have starches which act as thickeners, stabilisers and binders, making those products less nutritious per volume than the equivalent home prepared meal.

When buying commercial baby foods be aware of what they contain by reading the labels.

After a can of baby food has been opened, the unused portion should be transferred to a plastic or glass container and refrigerated. Never save uneaten food once it has been offered to the baby. The bacteria from the baby's saliva will contaminate the remaining food.

It is best to heat only the required amount. Reheating commercial baby foods can cause separation, which will affect the consistency and sometimes even the taste.

The uneaten portion of bottled baby food may be stored for 1-2 days in the original jar, if tightly closed; this is not safe if the whole jar has been offered to the baby.

Both canned and bottled baby foods can be heated in their containers, by immersing in a jug of boiling water. Bottled baby foods may also be heated, minus their lids, in a microwave oven.

A Word on Economy

While commercial baby food products are convenient, they can prove expensive. Compare the prices on regular lines of such products as unsweetened pie apples, peaches and plums, rice puddings, custards, and pure fruit juices. The regular products may require mashing or straining, but the difference in price can make this small chore worthwhile.

Fruit Jelly, Yoghurt Jelly and Junket (opposite)

PREPARING YOUR OWN BABY FOOD

The importance of good foods cannot be over-estimated. Even a busy mother can have a ready supply of home-prepared baby foods on hand. It requires a little organisation and planning.

The freezer provides the answer. If you do not have a freezer, the freezing compartment of a domestic refrigerator will keep food safely for several weeks.

It is more economical to prepare baby foods than to buy the equivalent, commercially prepared product, and it is just as convenient to serve home-prepared meals at home.

Baby food you prepare yourself does not contain any of the additives found in many commercially made foods, and therefore it offers more nutrients for the same weight. There is also a great deal of satisfaction to be gained from the knowledge that you are providing your child with a nourishing and balanced diet.

Where to Begin

When shopping, choose your ingredients wisely. Only the best fruits and vegetables in season. If you're buying unseasonal vegetables, take them only if they have been well stored, feel firm, fresh and bright in colour.

If you plan to process baby food in bulk for storage in the freezer, you will benefit from buying seasonal fruits and vegetables in quantity. Freeze some for baby, the remainder for yourself.

From time to time, make cost comparisons between commercially frozen fruits and vegetables and the available fresh product. You may be surprised to learn that standard frozen vegetables such as beans, peas, corn, cauliflower and broccoli are often less expensive than the fresh ones.

Always choose 'free flow' frozen vegetables. These have been frozen in trays so that the individual pieces do not stick together. If they are in a solid block chances are they have at some time defrosted and have begun to deteriorate. When opened, the pack can be resealed with freezer tape, or twist tie, but you may find it more convenient to transfer the contents to a plastic freezer box. You can then take just a handful as needed.

When buying meat, check the colour and general appearance. It should be bright with clear yellowish white fat. Meats which feel sticky or slimy or which have a slight colour should be avoided.

Storing Baby Foods

Prepared foods will keep safely for one to two days, even three in some instances, in the refrigerator. Heat only the amount to be served; keep the remainder cold.

Always keep food covered while it is in the refrigerator. Use small plastic containers to store foods separately. Discard all foods after two to three days.

The safe storage times of different food products vary. The instructions which accompanied your freezer should give accurate guidelines of its capabilities, but the following is a basic guide for freezing food for your baby.

1 week only: all kinds of fish

1 month: liver

2 months: combination dinners, cheese dishes, cream sauces

3 months: beef, lamb, veal, poultry, beans and peas

4 months: vegetables (excluding beans and peas)

6 months: fruits, juices and baked goods

Freezing: 'Food cube' method

Freezing baby foods in ice cube trays gives convenient one-meal sized portions. The trays should be thoroughly washed and rinsed before use, and when the cubes are solid, they can be transferred to plastic bags and returned to the freezer. Remember to label and date them clearly.

Remove only the number of food cubes needed for a meal, return unused cubes immediately to the freezer to prevent partial thawing which would result in their sticking together.

1 Spoon puree into ice-cube tray. Seal the tray into a clean plastic bag.

2 Once frozen, tip food cubes into the plastic bag. Label and date.

3 Transfer frozen cubes to plastic container. Label and date.

Freezing: 'Drop' method

Thoroughly clean a scone or biscuit tray. Place in the freezer to chill. When the food has been pureed or chopped, drop tablespoonfuls on to the tray. They will begin to freeze immediately, keeping their shape. Seal the tray into a clean plastic bag. Return to the freezer until solid, then remove and store in a labelled plastic bag.

Freezing can also be done in small Tupperware or other plastic containers such as yoghurt or cottage cheese tubs or take-away food tubs. Small plastic sandwich bags tied with wire twists are also suitable, but make sure that they are not placed directly on to the bottom of the freezer or they will stick to it.

1 Drop purée onto baking tray for freezing. Seal in plastic bag.

2 Transfer frozen drops to plastic container for freezing. Label and date.

3 Or transfer drops to plastic bag for freezing. Label and date.

Kitchen Equipment

There are several pieces of kitchen equipment which will make the preparation of baby foods easier.

- a food processor or blender is useful, but not essential.
- a pressure cooker is fast and efficient,
- a steamer also retains vitamins while cooking quickly, and
- a microwave oven cooks quickly.

If you have them, use them. If not, weigh their cost against their ability to save you valuable time.

Pressure cookers cook meats, fruits and vegetables quickly and efficiently while retaining most of the nutrients. They save electricity or gas as cooking times are drastically reduced.

As an alternative, steaming has become popular. It is quick, clean to the point of being sterile, and gives excellent results. Vegetables and fruits retain their goodness, colour, natural liquids and full flavour. Meats are rendered tender with excess fats drawn out.

A steamer insert to use in your own saucepans is inexpensive and can be found in most kitchenware shops. There are two types, the first being a shaped metal container with a wire handle, and many perforations around the sides and base. The collapsible kind is constructed on the fan principle with metal arms held together with wire.

If you decide to extend steaming to your own foods, you might decide to invest in a steamer. The Chinese model comes with several layers for cooking two or three dishes at one time. The saucepan type is similar to a double saucepan.

Heating Baby Foods

A double saucepan is ideal for thawing and heating frozen baby food cubes and drops. They can be placed in the saucepan straight from the freezer and then gently heated until warmed through. A small saucepan on very low heat also works well. A microwave oven thaws and warms in seconds.

Refrigerated foods can be warmed by placing the baby's food dish over a saucepan or jug of boiling water, or you may choose to purchase a warming dish — a plastic food dish with a water compartment below. This is filled with hot water and continues to warm the food.

1 Heat food cubes in double saucepan.

2 Heat food cubes in glass bowl over a saucepan of simmering water.

3 Put mixed food cubes in baby dish for reheating in microwave.

Tempting the Toddler's Taste Buds

You'll need plenty of patience and a good supply of facecloths during this stage. Your baby will start to make his own decisions about what he likes. It can be frustrating for both parent and child, but it is important to establish basic mealtime rules at this time. Our dietary plan for the toddler gives ideas and easy-to-prepare recipes for meals from breakfast through to supper.

Egg and Apricot Custard (page 49), Rice Pudding (page 49) and Apple Sago (page 49)   35

Give them what you want them to eat. Babies can't tell the difference, so long as it's nice and mushy. That is probably the most ill-informed advice I received when I was faced with a one-year-old who had already begun to voice her opinion on the subject.

Children do have taste buds. As toddlers, they may demand to exercise the inherent right to make up their own minds about what they like.

By now your baby will be a toddler. Mobile, more demanding and preferring to self-feed. The rate of progress will differ from child to child. Some are fiercely independent and impatient to get on with it by themselves. Others muddle messily through, and prefer the comforting personalised service offered with spoon feeding.

However the food actually reaches the mouth, once it gets there your determined young toddler will decide whether it's to go any further. You may find, to your dismay, your choicest culinary efforts being lobbed at the cat, or used to finger-paint the high chair. What your baby enjoyed yesterday may suddenly be 'yuk' today — a colourfully descriptive word which infants are wont to include in their early vocabulary. Its counterpart 'yum' will make an appearance at a later date.

This can be a particularly trying time for you. 'He/she was so good just a few weeks ago. Now nothing I cook is right,' you will wail. You'll agonise over menus, try to think up ways to decorate food to please them and generally work yourself into a state wondering what is wrong.

Probably nothing is wrong. Your child has just entered a stage which must be dealt with calmly.

To begin, do have a careful look at what you're preparing. Have you tended to remain in a rut, feeding something your baby liked at eight-months-old? Do you still mush the food into a thick and tasteless slurry? Are you over-estimating his ability to chew by offering large lumpy pieces? Is your baby teething?

If you feel that you're satisfied with the way you have been dealing with the situation to date then simply put his taste buds to the test. What nagging and anger will not achieve, other tactics might.

Try disguising the food you'd really like eaten by mixing in a favourite food, even if the combinations seem bizarre to you. My daughter found that spinach and peas ('yuk') were transformed into 'yum' when mashed and mixed in with her favourite, mashed potato. Her cousin accepted anything mixed with stewed apple.

A garnish such as sieved egg yolk over vegetables gives extra interest, a better taste and added nourishment.

If you're lucky your ruses will work. If not, the favourite food may now be rejected and you could be scraping your spinach souffle off the floor or stamping out to get yourself a soothing cup of tea.

Eating is not a Game

'Open wide, come inside... ', you chant ... 'Here comes the big green aeroplane ... ', attempts your spouse. 'Just one more bite and that's it ... ' you wheedle. Eating games are all very well. They work sometimes, but are they the sensible way to face up to the problem of an uninterested eater?

You might be prepared to sit with your child spooning each mouthful accompanied by cheery encouragement now. Are you still going to be so in a year's time if there has been no improvement? Making a game out of eating can result in your child remaining dependent on you for some years to come.

Discipline, gentle but firm, should help your child to gradually understand that eating is an important and necessary task, not a game. It's to be enjoyed, but not to be made into a time for playing catch with a handful of mashed potato.

The high chair will have become a place to sit in and play for hours. It is wise, however, to help your child distinguish quite clearly the difference between such playtime — with or without finger foods to nibble on — and meal times.

At this stage, the child should begin to join the family at some meals, if this has not been happening already. Older children must be discouraged from playing with the child during meal times, and discipline of their own activities is obviously essential.

Take stock of your own table manners, too. Have you developed some sloppy habits you'd prefer your child not to pick

Once children are mobile do not be tempted to give them food 'on the run'. Children need to sit down and be quiet while eating, not only for the benefit of social graces but also to lessen the risk of choking. Eating in a moving car also presents the risk of choking if there is a sudden change in motion, such as braking or swerving.

James was a red engine who lived at a station at the other end of the line. He had two small wheels in front and six driving wheels behind.

up? It's surprising how quickly youngsters begin to participate in the sport of testing your tolerance of bad behaviour.

During the day don't expect your baby to quietly eat alone. We like to eat in company, and you'll find your child does too. Keep him by your side while he's eating. Make his lunchtime yours, if you're at home alone; or save such stationary chores as ironing, dish washing and bringing the house accounts up to date, for his meal times. You can keep on with your tasks; he'll enjoy your company and the odd word from you, or help with a difficult piece of food.

You will enjoy your own evening meals more if your child has been fed, bathed and got ready for bed before you sit down. Older children or your spouse can then occupy the baby with bedtime stories while you put the finishing touches to your meal.

Yet evenings may be the only time during the week that father can be with his child, and you may prefer that they are together during your meal. If you eat early enough, your child will enjoy sitting with

you in his high chair. Satisfied with his dinner, he should be content with his favourite toy or piece of finger food, and keep himself happily occupied.

A Balanced Diet for the Toddler

The rapidly growing toddler requires plenty of protein for growth, carbohydrates and fats for energy, and to carry fat-soluble vitamins through the body.

The basic food requirements each day are (servings amount to about 2 tablespoons):

2–3 cups (500–750 mL) of milk (to be drunk and made into foods)

3–4 servings of whole grains or cereals

1–2 servings of meat, poultry, fish, eggs, nuts or beans (including peanut butter)

3–4 servings of vegetables and/or fruits*, including at least one serving high in vitamin C, eg. citrus, berries, tomato, capsicum, broccoli.

In the form of whole fruit and juice. Do not give juice exclusively as it is high in sugar and the pulp of citrus fruits contains fibre and other important elements.

Steamed Egg in a Nest (page 44)

Muesli, Boiled Eggs and French Toast (page 43)

The individual food requirements of children vary. Some will have very healthy appetites; others seem to thrive on far less. Your own child's size and degree of daily activity, as well as his own particular interest in eating, will help to determine how much he needs each day.

The best way to assess your child's requirements is to note the incidence of illness, times of apparent lethargy and frequency of disturbed nights.

If your child suffers infrequently or not at all from any of these, has plenty of energy for play, and generally appears healthy, happy and content, he's obviously well nourished.

Over-eating should be firmly discouraged. The quantities given above are perfectly adequate for a well-developed, active child in his second year. If your child seems to enjoy 'stuffing' his food, be firm and say no. Examine the possible reasons for his tendency.

Food Fads

If food fads and fancies are giving you concern, you'll have to try to come to grips with the problem. Certainly do not badger the child into eating just what you would like. If your child doesn't care for green vegetables this week, give yellow ones. If cereal is 'out' at present, offer whole grain or wholemeal bread, toast or crispbread. If yoghurt is a 'no-no' make milky puddings or creamy milk smoothies. Respect his individuality, up to a point.

A Balanced Diet

Examine his fad diet carefully. Even though the combination of his chosen foods may be unusual, you may be surprised to learn that they represent a reasonably well-balanced diet.

A balanced diet over a two to three week period will be better than one forced on the child each day. The overall effect of good eating habits is healthy progress. His ability and willingness to eat a wide variety of different foods is important in the long-term.

So if your child enjoys nothing but peanut butter sandwiches this week, simply make sure that the bread is wholemeal, and occasionally slip in a little creamed cottage cheese, alfalfa sprouts or a slice of tomato and watch the reaction to this innovation.

Next week he'll probably have a passion for mashed potato.

Keeping Up

Peer group psychology can be useful. At the times I've wanted to switch my daughter from a particular fad or to introduce a new food I suspected she wouldn't care for, I've invited her friends over for a tea party.

Invariably she would eat whatever was offered, so long as her friends ate it too. Though behavioural patterns in children of similar age tend to be reasonably consistent, food fads seem to be less so.

Side-stepping the Sweet Tooth Habit

In the formative months, your child will have begun to differentiate between sweet and salty tastes, though in infant foods neither would have been pronounced enough to have created preferences. As your baby's meals increasingly come to assume the tastes and consistency of adult meals, the flavours will be more distinct.

Sensibly, you may have taken the early precaution of alternating sweet dishes with savoury, rather than presenting a dessert at the end of each meal. You should also restrict the use of sweeteners and sweet finger foods, so the sweet-tooth habit should be reasonably well controlled.

As children get older, however, some do seem to like sweet tastes, and want them more as they grow. Given the choice, many 1–2 year olds will ask for a sweet food before a savoury one. Is it a natural habit, or one which has been conditioned by the various influences we are subjected to daily?

Well-meaning friends and relatives are often far too ready with a sweet biscuit or a piece of chocolate. Older children, television, glossy pictures in magazines and on billboards, and stocked supermarket shelves do insinuate their message into young minds.

Cultivating a sweet tooth is easy. Controlling one is more difficult, but not impossible.

Do you set a bad example yourself? Does your youngster see you sitting down to a large slice of cream cake or box of chocolates with your morning coffee? Do you cover your cereal with sugar every morning, or heap sugar into your tea? Do you keep a jar of jelly beans or chocolate drops in the pantry to use for keeping children quiet when you're on the telephone or as a reward?

With discipline you can drastically limit the amount of sugar your child consumes.

Don't keep sweets in the house, but offer fresh fruit, dried fruits (soaked or cooked until your child is old enough to have them straight from the packet), cheese cubes or crackers if you want to give a snack.

Make your own biscuits or cakes, using little sugar; or buy only low sugar crackers. Don't add sugar to cereals and use it sparingly yourself in tea and coffee.

Buy natural ice-creams and ice blocks, or make your own using full cream milk and diluted natural fruit juices. Don't offer dessert after every meal. Plain yoghurt, fruit or milk drinks are a good alternative. Avoid giving your child sweet carbonated drinks. Milk and water are the only beverages a young child needs.

If you must sweeten, use sugar or honey (there's no real difference between them) in moderation. Make your own jellies using fresh fruit juices and unflavoured, unsweetened gelatine.

Take a jar of your own mixture of dried fruits when visiting. Ask the host to offer these to your child instead of sweets.

Sugar, as well as damaging the teeth, upsets the body's natural balance. When eaten, it is instantly released into the bloodstream, giving a quick lift. The body's reaction is to release extra insulin from the pancreas to bring the blood sugar level down to normal. There is usually an over-reaction, however, causing the level to drop to a point lower than normal.

Additionally, the eating of excessive amounts of sweet foods has been linked with the incidence of hyperactivity in children.

You will be making a very responsible decision on your child's behalf by limiting his sugar intake. Its effects will be felt

Avoid spending hours preparing some exquisite dish, if you know your toddler is going through a 'picky' phase.

not just immediately, but also in years to come.

The Bottle can be Baby's Best Friend

'But it's my friend,' screamed my daughter when I announced after her second birthday that she was now old enough to do without her bottle.

Before beginning a battle royal over the issue, examine your own motives. Is it doing any harm? Can it be that you are simply embarrassed by this large toddler's obsession with a symbol of babyhood?

It has been agreed amongst dentists and paediatricians that sucking should have no lasting ill-effects on the formation of the gums, teeth or jaw. The sucking reflex is more important to some children than to others. They usually have a very personal motive for their dependence on the bottle, and it is often one of security.

In my circle of acquaintances, I've looked at the children who have not clung to their bottles. They have one thing in common: they all have a particular special thing, such as a soft toy, a scrap of cuddly cloth, or they suck their thumb or fingers, or twiddle with their hair. Each has a comforting habit or object which accompanies him everywhere. Several of these children were weaned from the breast to a cup, having only water or orange juice from a bottle, and therefore the bottle has never assumed any great importance in their lives.

The children who have clung to their bottles usually have no other possession of importance, nor other sucking habits. The bottle obviously fills the child's need to be comforted, and to possess.

If you do want to break the habit, do it gently. Begin to restrict the times he can have the bottle. Don't forcibly remove it, break it or throw it in the bin. You might find your toddler turning out the bin or trying to piece the bits back together in a flood of hysterical crying.

I did observe an element of self-consciousness about my daughter's use of her bottle after this second birthday, though. She took to 'not wanting a bottle tonight, Mummy' whenever we had visitors or if we were staying with friends. The next step was to need a bottle, filled with milk or juice, to hold while she went

Macaroni Cheese (page 48) and vegetables

to sleep. Eventually she decided that she would lend it to her doll — just for a while. Recently I've seen her occasionally sucking her thumb.

Meals for Toddlers

Your toddler will be now eating more or less the same sort of food you prepare for the family.

With a little organisation cooking should not mean separate preparation, cooking time or equipment.

Family casseroles, stews, bolognaise sauce and even mild curries will usually be enjoyed by the toddler. Large portions can be cut into manageable pieces at the time of serving.

Don't cook a hot meal especially for the child if the family is having a cold one. There are plenty of cold meats, boiled eggs and salad ingredients he can enjoy.

A cooked or cold cereal for breakfast, with perhaps an egg or toast, a cold lunch and a cooked dinner is the meal-time pattern for most families. The toddler can fit into this system happily.

I've found that a mini midday meal is ideal for both myself and my daughter. It can be made up of whatever is on hand, takes minutes to prepare and is a delicious, low kilojoule meal. The refrigerator usually yields a little cold meat, a piece of fruit, some sticks of cheese and vegetables. There's always a tin of salmon or tuna in the pantry, and eggs to be hard-boiled and pepped up with a dot of mayonnaise. If I add a few olives for myself, Isobel gets a couple of raisins or a dried apricot.

Cereals

Select on the best high-fibre, sugar-free types of dry cereal and serve them without

Be very very careful with nuts. Children up to the age of seven have died from choking on whole peanuts, so the medical profession advises you to avoid whole or chopped nuts for as long as possible. Even crushed nuts and crunchy peanut butter can cause choking and coughing.

added sugar, honey or other sweetener.

Alternatively, make your own cereals and muesli. They offer good nutritional value. Old-fashioned oatmeal (rolled oats), and cream of wheat (semolina) are tasty, warming and sustaining, particularly good for the colder months. Another delicious, nutty-flavoured home-made cereal can be made with brown rice. Give cereals zip by adding:

- chopped dried fruits,
- honey or treacle swirled in patterns,
- a spoonful of raw or toasted wheatgerm,
- puréed or chopped fruits — canned, fresh or cooked,
- a teaspoon or two of milk powder to make it extra creamy,
- a teaspoon of butter — drop into the centre to melt, then swirl around, or
- a few spoonfuls of muesli, bran flakes or other bran cereal.

Hot Brown Rice Cereal

Grind ¼ cup (60 g) of raw brown rice to a reasonably fine powder in a food processor or blender. Pour into a saucepan and add a small pinch of salt (optional), 2 teaspoons of milk powder and 1 cup (250 mL) of milk (or use half milk and half water). Bring to the boil and simmer, stirring occasionally, for about 10 minutes.

Any whole grains, fine ground before use, are suitable as cooked cereal. Simply simmer in milk or milk and water combined, until tender. Try oats, wheat, corn or millet, or buy pre-ground grain meal where health foods are sold.

Home-made Muesli

Mix any of the following items in quantities to suit your own taste: raw oatmeal, wheatgerm (toasted or raw), bran, raisins, sultanas (seedless raisins), currants, chopped dried apricots, chopped dried apple, cracked or whole wheat, millet, dried milk powder, honey.

For the toddler, grind the components to a powder. Serve with milk or simmer briefly in milk to soften.

Making your own baby foods is creative, inexpensive and healthy — rewarding both parent and baby. However, on those days when you need a break, give yourself a holiday and buy a little convenience food in a can — it won't harm the child and it can give you a change of routine.

Vegetables

Spinach and Potato

Peel and boil 1 medium potato until tender. Cook 1 tablespoon of finely chopped fresh or frozen spinach with 2 teaspoons of water and 1 teaspoon butter in a small saucepan over very low heat, for 4 minutes. Keep the pan tightly covered during cooking, then drain to remove excess liquid. Mash the potato and stir in the spinach.

Peas, broccoli and chopped lettuce can be used in place of the spinach.

Steamed Vegetables with White Sauce

Prepare 2–3 teaspoons each of finely diced carrots, frozen peas, sliced green beans and small sprigs of cauliflower or broccoli. Place in a dish and add 1 tablespoon of water. Steam until tender, about 10 minutes for harder vegetables, or microwave in a covered dish for 2–3 minutes. Drain, add 2 tablespoons of *White Sauce* (page 48) and heat through.

Vegetable Patty

Beat an egg or egg yolk into any leftover steamed or boiled green, yellow or white vegetables, pour into a small dish and steam until the egg is set. Alternatively, you can fry it in a small frying pan with 1 teaspoon of butter.

Creamed Potato or Parsnip

Boil 1 medium peeled potato or young parsnip until very tender. Mash with 1 teaspoon milk and 1 teaspoon ricotta cheese or dry milk powder.

Cheesy Potatoes

Cook 1 medium peeled potato until tender. Mash with a little milk, then stir in 1 teaspoon of finely grated cheese and ½ teaspoon butter.

Vegetable Casserole

In a small ovenproof dish with a lid, place 1 small peeled potato, cubed, 1 peeled carrot, sliced, 2 teaspoons frozen or fresh peas, 2–3 cubes peeled parsnip, sweet potato (yam), squash or zucchini (courgettes). Cover with water and place the dish in a moderate oven 180°C (350°F/Gas 4) to cook, covered, until the vegetables are tender, about 30 minutes. Add more water, if needed, during cooking. This cooks in minutes in a microwave.

Eggs

Boiled Eggs

Place an egg in a small saucepan with cold water to cover. Bring to the boil, reduce the heat slightly and time the cooking from when the first bubbles break the surface to eleven minutes. Remove, rinse in cold water and place in an egg cup. Remove the top of the egg immediately.

Some ideas:
- knit or buy a woollen egg cosy
- paint eyes and a big smile on the shell of the egg with a marker pen
- add a few drops of food colouring to the water to dye the egg a bright colour
- serve with fingers of butter wholemeal bread or toast for dipping.

Cheesy Scramble

Lightly beat 1 egg with 1 teaspoon ricotta or cottage cheese, or grated soft cheese and 2 teaspoons milk. Melt 1 teaspoon butter in a small frying pan and pour in the egg. Cook over moderate heat, stirring occasionally, until just set.
- Use a gingerbread man cutter or fancy biscuit cutters to cut toast into fun shapes.

Fluffy Omelette

Lightly beat 1 egg yolk with 1 teaspoon of water. Beat the whites of 2 eggs to soft peaks and stir in the yolk. Melt 1 teaspoon butter in a small pan and pour in the omelette. Cook quickly on one side, then turn and cook until just firm.
- Fillings of cooked flaked fish chopped sautéed onions, mushrooms, tomato or kidney, or grated cheese can be used. Place along the centre of the omelette on the uncooked side, then fold over, cook until cooked through, turn once.

Traditional French Toast

Lightly butter the bread, dip into beaten egg and fry in butter until golden. Sprinkle orange or lemon juice, add a pinch of cinnamon, then dust lightly with icing (confectioners') sugar.
- Cut bread into the shape of a cat face

Meatloaf (page 46)

by trimming away the lower corners of slice to make rounded cheeks and a pointed chin. Then shape the top edge into a rounded head with two pointed ears. Dip into egg and fry in butter to make French Toast, then add halved dried apricots for eyes, a few raisins for the nose and a strip of orange rind for the mouth.

Egg Custard

Beat 1 egg lightly with 2 teaspoons milk and a pinch of cornflour (corn-starch). Add a little honey or sugar as preferred. Pour into a small heatproof dish or teacup (a porcelain Chinese teacup is ideal) and steam until set, about 6 minutes.

For variety, add minced cooked chicken, turkey, veal or liver, flaked cooked fish, chopped cooked vegetables, or any combinations of these, to unsweetened custard to make a tasty quick meal.

Steamed Egg in a Nest

Mash 1 medium cooked potato with a little butter or milk and spread in the bottom of a small greased ramekin. Spread 2 tablespoons of chopped cooked spinach on top and make a slight depression in the centre. Break an egg into this, cover the dish; bake or steam until the egg is firm, about 6 minutes for steaming, 15 minutes for baking; microwave 2 minutes.

This makes a delightful first course for your own meals. For extra flavour, cover cooked egg with 1 tablespoon *White Sauce* (page 48) and coat with grated cheese. Pop under a very hot grill until the cheese has melted and browned slightly.

Fish

Select fresh white fish, avoiding the darker, more oily kinds as these have a strong flavour which your child may not appreciate. Remove the skin from fillets by placing skin side down on a board. Dip the fingers of the left hand into salt to give a better grip and press firmly down on the tail. Use a narrow bladed sharp knife to scrape and roll the meat from the skin. Rub the fingers along the fillet on both sides to check for bones.

Fish for the toddler can be poached by simmering in water to cover at a temperature just below the boil, until tender, about 4 minutes; steamed in a dish over boiling water; put under a moderate grill; or shallow fried in a little butter or oil.

Fish Kedgeree

Cut a 90 g piece of fish into small cubes and place in a lightly greased small ramekin with 2 tablespoons of cooked rice, 2 teaspoons each of frozen peas and parboiled diced carrot and ¾ cup (185 mL) milk. Add ½ teaspoon chopped parsley and stir in lightly. Simmer gently or bake in a moderate oven 180°C (350°F/ Gas 4) until the vegetables are tender.

Steamed Fish and Vegetable Cake

Finely chop about 185 g of fish and mix with 1 beaten egg. Spoon half into a small buttered dish and cover with 90 g of finely diced or mashed cooked vegetables. Cover with the remaining fish and smooth the top using a wet spoon. Set the dish in a steamer and steam for about 15 minutes until the fish is firm.

Tuna Egg Breakfast

Mix 1 tablespoon of drained and flaked canned tuna with 1 tablespoon mashed potato and 1 beaten egg. Melt 2 teaspoons butter in a small frying pan and pour in the mixture. Cook until lightly coloured on the underside, turn and cook the other side until the egg is set.

Tuna Patties

Mix together 3 tablespoons of drained and flaked canned tuna (or salmon), 1 beaten egg, 2 tablespoons fresh brown breadcrumbs or mashed potato, 1 teaspoon lemon juice and 1 teaspoon finely chopped parsley. Squeeze the ingredients through the fingers until thoroughly mixed and slightly sticky. Form into balls using wet hands and flatten into patties. Shallow fry in a mixture of vegetable oil and butter until golden. Drain and serve.

Fish patties can also be made in the same way, using flaked cooked fish or smoked fish.

In summer, you may find your toddler drinks far more than he or she eats. Considering that the human body is composed of 90% fluids, this is perfectly natural. In the cool of the evening, however, you may persuade your child to eat some chilled soup, fresh salad, a little cold meat or hard-boiled egg, to ensure a correct balance of nutrients is maintained.

A great white
Is sailing,
Is sailing
Down to sea.

during the evening. His mother put him to bed,

Fish Kedgeree (opposite), Steamed Chicken Meatballs with Spinach and Potato (page 46) and Tuna Patties (opposite)

Chicken

Chicken Liver Pâté

In a small saucepan with 1 tablespoon butter, gently sauté 90 g of fresh chicken livers with about 45 g of chopped chicken until cooked through. Add 2 tablespoons of milk and 1 teaspoon of cornflour and simmer, stirring, for 2 minutes. Transfer to a blender or food processor and purée. Pour into small dishes and refrigerate. Serve with fingers of buttered bread or toast.

Steamed Chicken Meatballs

Finely mince a half chicken breast after removing skin and bone. Mix with 1½ tablespoons fresh breadcrumbs and half a beaten egg. Squeeze the mixture through the fingers until thoroughly mixed and smooth, then use wet hands to form it into small meatballs. Thoroughly wash several lettuce or spinach leaves and shred finely. Arrange in a small dish and set the meatballs on top. Place the dish in a steamer and steam for about 9 minutes. Purée the vegetables with 1 tablespoon *White Sauce* (page 48), serve separately.

● Steam small cubes of potato in the same pot to serve with the meatballs. Add a few drops of lemon juice to the meatball mixture for extra flavour.

Steamed Chicken Breast and Apple

Cut ¼–½ chicken breast, skinned and boned, into small cubes and place in a dish. Peel, core and slice half a red apple and arrange over the chicken. Set the dish in a steamer and steam until tender, about 7 minutes. Purée or chop, serve together.

Chicken, Rice and Vegetable Timbales

In small containers (aluminium cups or Chinese teacups) layer small portions of cooked chopped or pureed chicken, cooked rice and cooked mixed vegetables (carrots, peas, broccoli, squash), moistening each layer with a teaspoon of *White Sauce* (page 48) or milk. Pour half a beaten egg into the top of each cup and cover with aluminium foil. Bake in a bain marie in a moderate oven 180°C (350°F/Gas 4) for 25–30 minutes, or steam for 10–12 minutes. Unmould before serving. Refrigerate the uneaten timbales for up to 3 days.

Meat

Veal Hotpot

Select a meaty slice of veal shank with the bone intact and place in a small casserole with 1 large chopped tomato, 1 teaspoon finely chopped parsley, a piece of bay leaf and water to cover. Cover the casserole. Bake in a moderate oven 180°C (350°F/Gas 4) for about 45 minutes. Add more water to the casserole during cooking as needed. Scrape the meat from the shank bone before serving, and stir in additional chopped parsley and a tiny pinch of finely grated lemon peel.

Braised Beef and Vegetables

Cut 90 g of good stewing beef into small cubes and place them in a small casserole with 1 new potato, a small carrot, a small stick of celery, 1 pickling onion, a piece of bay leaf and a sprig of parsley. Add water to cover and cook in a moderate oven 180°C (350°F/Gas 4) for about 45 minutes. Add more water as needed. Remove the meat and vegetables, discard the bay leaf and parsley, and chop or purée, then return to the sauce. Thicken if desired with a mixture of cornflour and cold water.

● An excellent beef and vegetable soup can be prepared in the same way as above, using more water and adding tomato juice to taste.

Meatloaf

Finely mince 185 g of lean beef and sauté in a little butter with 1 finely chopped spring onion. Remove from the heat and add 1 chopped tomato, 2 tablespoons of cooked diced carrots and 1 tablespoon of cooked peas, 1 beaten egg, 2 tablespoons of breadcrumbs and 1 teaspoon of chopped parsley. Press the mixture into a lightly greased dish or several pie containers and cover with strips of streaky bacon. Bake in a preheated moderate oven 180°C (350°F/Gas 4) for about 30 minutes.

Try to introduce salads early — they are a busy parent's godsend. Fresh, delicious, healthy ingredients take only a few minutes to prepare, involve no cooking and offer plenty of fibre and vitamins. They can be as simple as fresh cucumber, or you can go on adding little bits and pieces: fresh fruit, canned fish such as tuna or salmon, boiled egg, capsicum, cheese cubes, carrot sticks, celery diagonals and so on.

White Lamb Stew

Cut a thick slice of boneless leg lamb into cubes. Peel and dice 1 small onion and place in a casserole with the lamb and 1 tablespoon fresh or frozen peas. Cover with a mixture of milk and water and add a sprig of parsley and a piece of bay leaf. Simmer gently or bake in a moderate oven 180°C (350°F/Gas 4) for about 40 minutes until the meat is tender. Thicken the sauce with a mixture of cornflour and cold water.

A tablespoon of plain yoghurt, cream cheese or fresh cream adds flavour.

Cottage Pie

Brown 155 g of lean minced meat and 1 finely chopped small onion in 1 tablespoon butter, then add 1½ tablespoons of finely diced vegetables (carrots, peas, turnips, squash, pumpkin). Cover with water or beef stock and simmer for about 20 minutes, adding additional water if it is needed. Thicken the sauce with a mixture of cornflour and cold water. Boil 2 medium potatoes and mash them with a little milk. Transfer the meat to a small heatproof dish and cover it with the mashed potato. Mix 2 teaspoons of grated soft cheese and 2 teaspoons of breadcrumbs together and sprinkle over the potato. Dot with butter, grill lightly.

Steak and Kidney Casserole

Brown 155 g of lean minced beef or veal and 1 finely chopped small onion in 1 tablespoon butter. Skin 2 sheep's kidneys and remove the white cores. Dice and brown with the meat. Sprinkle 2 teaspoons flour over the meat and cook lightly, then add 2 small chopped tomatoes and 5–6 chopped fresh mushrooms and a piece of bay leaf. Add water or beef stock to cover and 1 teaspoon of chopped parsley. Simmer or bake in a moderate oven 180°C (350°F/Gas 4) until tender, about 30 minutes.

Soup

Beef Tea

Place 1 kg of meaty beef bones in a large casserole with a lid, add 5 cups (1.25 L) water, 1 bay leaf and a spring onion. Cover the casserole and set it on a rack in a steamer. Steam for 4 hours, topping up the water as needed. This gentle slow cooking will extra all the goodness from the meat and bones.

Use beef tea as the base for soups, gravies and sauces.

Chicken Stock

Cook chicken bones or carcasses from roast chicken or uncooked chickens in the same way as beef tea is prepared, to make a rich white chicken stock. Alternatively, simply place the bones in a saucepan with plenty of water, a bay leaf and an onion; simmer about 1½ hours, then strain.

These recipes make enough for mother or father as well.

Italian Egg Soup

Mix 1½ cups (375 mL) of beef tea with ⅓ cup (75 mL) tomato juice and heat to boiling. Remove from the heat. Break 2 eggs into a cup and slide into the soup. Leave to poach gently in the hot soup. Add a sprinkling of grated Parmesan or other choose and 1 teaspoon finely chopped parsley.

Vegetable Soup

Simmer 2 tablespoons of finely diced vegetables in 2 cups (500 mL) of beef tea or chicken stock until tender. Blend to a smooth purée and serve with grilled cheese on toast.

Chicken Noodle Soup

In 1⅓ cups (440 mL) of chicken stock, poach 60 g of finely minced chicken, 2–3 slices of spring onion and 1 tablespoon of broken egg noodles for 5–7 minutes. Add ½ teaspoon chopped parsley before serving.

Egg Flower Soup

Use 1½–2 cups (500 mL) of liquid from poaching fish and add 2 tablespoons minced (ground) raw or flaked cooked fish. Heat through, then remove from the heat and slowly add 2 lightly beaten eggs

Soup is another marvellous snack food that can make life easy for the adult, offering good nutrition, wonderful variety, speed and convenience. It even comes in tins, for those times when you're back at work or simply feeling tired.

and ½ teaspoon chopped parsley. Do not stir the soup until the egg has set in fine strands.

Cream of Spinach Soup

Bring 1¾ cups (440 mL) of milk to the boil and add 1 teaspoon of butter, 125 g fresh or frozen spinach and a pinch of nutmeg. Simmer for 5–6 minutes, then purée in a blender.

● Cook grated carrot, sprigs of broccoli or finely diced celery in the same way.

Beef and Vegetable Soup

Simmer 2–3 tablespoons of finely diced vegetables in 2 cups (500 mL) of beef tea with 60 g of lean minced beef, until the vegetables and meat are tender, and break apart easily.

Rice and Pasta

Rice Cooking

Wash the rice in one lot of cold water and drain well. Add 1¾ cups (440 mL) of water to each cup (155 g) of rice. Bring to the boil, cover tightly and then reduce the heat to the lowest point possible. Leave to steam gently until all of the liquid is absorbed and the rice is tender and fluffy, about 20 minutes.

Cooked rice freezes superbly. Store small amounts in plastic bags for quick baby meals.

Steamed Chicken Rice

Cook rice as directed above. When the rice is half cooked and the water is below the level of the rice, place diced uncooked chicken and a few sprigs of broccoli or cauliflower on the rice. Re-cover and cook until the rice is tender and the meat and vegetables cooked through.

Tomato and Fish Rice

Mix 2 tablespoons of cooked rice with 2 tablespoons flaked white fish and add a finely chopped cherry tomato and 1 teaspoon softened butter. Turn into a small dish, cover with aluminium foil and steam for about 8 minutes.

When you first introduce your toddler to eating at a restaurant, try to choose a family-run concern that enjoys serving children. It helps if there is a fish tank or some other object kids can look at. Some marvellous restaurants provide special play rooms for young children to rage around in, while their parents take a welcome break.

Pasta Cooking

Bring a saucepan of water to the boil and add 1 teaspoon butter or vegetable oil. Drop in the pasta and cook just below boiling point until very tender. Pasta cooked for young children must be softer than that suitable for adults. Mash or chop it finely before serving.

Macaroni Cheese

Boil 60 g macaroni until it is tender. Drain and place in a small greased dish and stir in 1 tablespoon of finely grated soft cheese and 1 teaspoon dry milk powder. Add ¾ cup (185 mL) of milk and cover with aluminium foil. Bake in a moderate oven 180°C (350°F/Gas 4) for about 30 minutes, or steam for 15 minutes.

Spaghetti with Meat Sauce

Cook 60 g of broken spaghetti in boiling water until tender. Drain and mix with 1 teaspoon butter. Sauté 60 g of lean minced beef or veal for 2–3 minutes in 1 tablespoon butter, then add tomato juice to cover. Simmer until the meat is tender, about 15 minutes. Pour over the spaghetti, garnish with 1 teaspoon grated cheese.

Cheesy Noodles

Cook 60 g of egg noodles until tender. Drain, add 1 teaspoon butter, 1 tablespoon grated cheese and 1 tablespoon milk. Mix well, heat over a saucepan of boiling water. Stir in a little chopped parsley.

Cheese Sauce

Make a *White Sauce* (see following recipe), then add 1–2 tablespoons grated soft cheese and a pinch of nutmeg.

White Sauce

Melt 2–3 teaspoons butter in a small saucepan, add 1 tablespoon flour. Cook for 1 minute. Bring 1 cup (250 mL) of milk to the boil, pour over the flour mixture. Boil, stirring briskly, until thickened.

Sweet Tastes

Apple Banana Bake

Thinly slice a peeled apple or banana and

arrange it in the bottom of a well buttered oven dish. Sprinkle 1 teaspoon (optional) of honey or sugar over the fruit and pour 1 well-beaten egg over it. Cover with aluminium foil and bake in a slow oven 150°C (300°F/Gas 2) for about 30 minutes. Remove the foil after 15 minutes to allow the top to brown lightly.

Apple Sago

Heat 1 cup of milk until it is almost boiling, then sprinkle in 15 g of sago and simmer, stirring, for about 10 minutes. Thinly slice an apple and arrange in the bottom of a buttered oven dish. Pour on the sago and dot with 1 teaspoon butter. Cover with aluminium foil and bake in a preheated modern oven 180°C (350°F/ Gas 4) for about 20 minutes.

Egg and Apricot Custard

Mix 1 beaten egg with 2 teaspoons milk and 2 teaspoons puréed apricot (or peach, apple or plum). Pour into a custard cup or teacup and set in a steamer. Cover and steam over gently boiling water until set, about 10 minutes.

Rice Pudding

Place 1 tablespoon of short grain rice in a small saucepan and add 1 teaspoon butter and 1 cup (250 mL) milk. Cover tightly and simmer until the rice is completely tender, or bake in a moderate oven 180°C (350°F/Gas 4) for about 45 minutes. Stir in 2 teaspoons of brown sugar or drizzle on a little honey to sweeten.

Semolina Pudding

This can be made in the same way as rice pudding, using semolina (cream of wheat) instead of the rice.

Frozen Fruit Yoghurt

Purée ½ cup (60 g) fresh fruit salad (pineapple, apple, banana, peach, apricot, orange) and mix with ½ cup (125 g) plain yoghurt. Pour into a freezer tray and freeze.

For a lighter texture, remove from the freezer, whip in the blender and then refreeze. Repeat once.

Apple Banana Bake and Frozen Fruit Yoghurt

FEEDING PROBLEMS AND ALLERGIES

Teething can be a trying time for both baby and mother. Cooling foods help to reduce a high temperature and soothe sore gums. Fruits, pudding, gelatine desserts and cottage cheese are ideal to substitute for regular meals during the worst days, as these dishes are cool and light.

Try offering a frozen peeled banana, or place a dummy (pacifier) in the freezer until it's icy cold. Your baby will appreciate the coldness on his gums, and will be able to exercise the gnawing reflex, which seems to work overtime while baby is teething.

Illness and fever can cause your child to lose interest in eating. It is advisable to consult your doctor if the symptoms last for more than a few hours, and do not appear to be teething related.

The importance of fluids cannot be overstressed in times such as these. Water, diluted fruit juice or well-crushed ice are soothing and help to lower his temperature as well as prevent dehydration, which can result in delirium, and a worsening of the illness.

You don't feel much like eating when you're ill, and baby usually responds in the same way. Don't

worry unduly. He won't starve in just a few days, so avoid offering his regular milk if there is any indication that he is being upset by it.

When he begins to feel better offer easy-to-digest foods like custard, junket, jellies and soft-boiled eggs, or hard-boiled egg yolks mashed with milk. Don't force him to eat. He'll be ravenous once the fever subsides and will soon make up for the few days loss of nourishment by eating everything in sight.

Intolerance to food can develop at any age, and can be hereditary,

though the allergies within one family need not necessarily have the same cause. The symptoms include spots or rashes on the skin, vomiting, diarrhoea, runny nose, wheezing and coughing, or asthma. Two symptoms often attributed to allergy are a continual watery nasal discharge and a persistent cough which lasts for more than two weeks. As these symptoms are similar to those of the common cold, it would be unwise to automatically assume an allergy and to begin any kind of home treatment. It is always best to consult your doctor.

If you have been introducing new foods at regular intervals, it may be reasonably easy to isolate an allergy-inducing food and to eliminate it from the baby's diet.

Foods which most commonly produce an allergic reaction include cow's milk, eggs (particularly egg whites), wheat, orange juice, strawberries, prawns and related shellfish, chocolate, peanuts and artificial food colourings. The first four items on the list will be offered to the baby in this second half year, and should be introduced gradually and immediately withdrawn if any symptoms occur. The latter foods can be avoided until the child is well into his second year, or even later, and is better able to deal with allergies. Whole or chopped nuts should not be given to children under seven years.

Many food allergies do occur continually through a person's lifetime, making it necessary to avoid the particular food at all times. Allergies can be serious. Always consult your doctor about how to deal with the problem. If you are able to give a reasonably accurate assessment of which foods appear to be affecting the child, you will be assisting in seeking a cure, and in establishing a diet that avoids your child's problems.

Some children are allergic to cow's milk, making it impossible to wean them from breast to most formulas as well as cow's milk. For such cases, soy bean milk may be the answer. Some children may be allergic to both cow's milk and soy. Once again, consult your doctor. Children at risk of developing allergies have fewer problems if they are breast fed.

Into the Third Year

Adding interest to children's meal times is just as important for the parents as for the child. As children grow, you can encourage them to be receptive to new tastes. By balancing nutritional necessities with interesting flavours you can establish good eating patterns, which will last through their lives.

Baked Chicken and Rice-filled Tomato Cases (page 58), Asparagus in Cream Sauce (page 55) and Bean Bundles (page 55)   53

Introducing Egg, Fish and Peanuts

Only a small percentage of babies are prone to being allergic to these foods. Babies who show signs of allergies or come from allergic families are those at greatest risk of having allergic reactions to any milk protein, soy protein, egg, wheat, fish and peanuts. These foods are better left to be tried after the age of one year in such children. If there is a family history in either parent or a sibling of allergies to these substances then the baby has a high risk of being allergic too, and the family history should be heeded before choosing a time to introduce these foods.

Eggs are such convenient nutritious food that they should be introduced if there are no risk factors around the seventh month in the same way that other foods are introduced — 1 teaspoon the first day, a few the next and then continue feeding if there are no problems, but then wait at least three days before trying another new food. Allergies sometimes show up at the first feed, but it may be on the second or third feeding that reactions occur.

Fish can cause reactions for two possible reasons. It can cause true allergic reactions or reactions from the high natural chemical content present in all but the freshest of white-flesh fish. Without a history of risk factors, some time around ten months is the time to introduce boneless fish. The natural chemicals in tasty fish, such as salmon and tuna, are similar to those in cheese and chocolate, and they are best avoided until well into the second year.

Peanuts are best avoided in children until seven years. In those without allergy risk factors, only smooth peanut butter is appropriate in the smallest amount in a sandwich. Peanuts and peanut butter have properties that cause them to easily stick in the back of the mouth, which can cause gagging and choking. If inhaled, they cause problems not only because of blocking the airway but also because of inflammation around the area where they lodge in the airway if the child survives the initial choking episode.

Cereals that contain gluten (wheat, barley, oats and rye) are best not introduced until six or seven months, although some babies thrive without ill-effect on cereals containing wheat from around four months. The delay is advised because of the suspected potential of the immature bowel to become sensitive to gluten and which will lead to coeliac disease. Families with a known history of coeliac disease should seek the advice of a paediatrician.

THE SECOND BIRTHDAY IS A LAND-MARK. No longer a baby, your child will have gained a certain mastery over her body and mind and will have begun to grow up. The child will be able to speak well enough to convey basic thoughts and wants and will be experimenting with a knife and fork.

Some children achieve mastery over eating implements much faster than others. Early opportunities to practice with a spoon will encourage the development of coordination. Regular cutlery is too big for toddlers to control.

There are several types of junior knife and fork sets marketed today which have handles specially moulded to accommodate small hands. These will give confidence and make the actual manipulation easier. Your child should also be able to drink quite confidently from a cup or glass. You may still prefer to avoid accidents by using a training cup, or by purchasing one of the covered cups with straws. Thin soups are best served in a cup; thick soups can be eaten with a spoon.

It is desirable to continue with a well-balanced diet of the same components as were listed for the one-year-old. Depending on your child's needs, the amount of each serving can be increased to 75–90 g.

Milk still offers the growing child much food value and should not be ignored. Many children go off milk as a drink but happily eat it as cheese, yoghurt, custard or on cereal. Encourage the child to drink 5–6 glasses of water, milk and diluted fruit juice.

You may find that her appetite is smaller than in the previous year. At two years of age, your child may enter a period of slower growth and this can account for apparent loss of appetite.

But consult your doctor if your child continues with a small appetite for a long period, combined with a drop in energy.

Try to enjoy a children's party. Invite your own mother along for moral support (and physical help), provide some tea or coffee for any other mothers, and remember the noise level will eventually die down.

Meals for the Whole Family

Your child will now be eating foods which are lightly seasoned or spiced but may not yet have developed a palate for some of the well-seasoned or highly spiced foods which we might enjoy.

The recipes in this section are for family meals which can be served to the child. In some, the child's portion will need to be cooked separately; others will be lightly seasoned and the remaining seasonings added after serving the child's portion.

Vegetables

Vegetables need never be a dull accompaniment to your meals. Here are some simple ideas to pep up a variety of vegetable dishes.

Vegetables

Bean Bundles

250 g green (French) beans
1 spring onion
white pepper
butter

Remove tips from beans and boil in water or steam until tender. Drain, add a dash of white pepper and a small nut of butter. Cut off the long green leaves of the spring onion and cut lengthways into strips. Divide the beans into 4 bundles and tie each with a strip of spring onion.

Creamed Spinach

500 g fresh or frozen spinach or silverbeet
1 tablespoon butter
cream
1/3 teaspoon ground nutmeg

Finely chop fresh spinach after washing three times in clean cold water. Thaw and thoroughly drain frozen spinach if it is used. Melt the butter in a saucepan and add the spinach. Cover tightly and simmer for 6–7 minutes, then drain the spinach thoroughly. Add the cream and nutmeg to taste.

Asparagus in Cream Sauce

1 × 340 g can green asparagus spears or tips
2 teaspoons butter
2 teaspoons flour
3/4 cup (185 mL) milk
1 tablespoon cream
1 egg yolk

Heat asparagus in its liquid, then drain and arrange on a serving dish. Melt butter in a small saucepan and add the flour. Stir for 1 minute, then pour in the milk. Stir over moderate heat until the sauce is thick and then remove it from the heat. Mix the cream and egg yolk together and beat them into the sauce. Pour the sauce over the asparagus and serve at once.

Zucchini Boats

4 small zucchini (courgettes)
1 thick slice pumpkin
1 tablespoon cream

Wipe the zucchini and use a small sharp knife to remove a strip along the length of each. Hollow out the centres without damaging the cases. Drop into boiling water and simmer until almost tender. Drain and place on an oven tray. Peel and dice the pumpkin and boil or steam until very tender. Drain thoroughly and pass through a fine sieve to remove any fibres. Add the cream. Spoon the pumpkin mixture into a piping bag with a large star nozzle. Pipe the mixture into the zucchini shells. Bake in a very hot oven 240°C (475°F/Gas 9) for about 7 minutes before serving.

● Button squash can also be prepared in this way. Cut off the pointed end and scoop out a small portion of the inside. Pipe the pumpkin into a rosette.

Bubble and Squeak

1 cup each cooked leftover potato, cabbage, pumpkin or squash, broccoli or peas (or other vegetables)
3 eggs, beaten
2 finely chopped chives
1 tablespoon butter

Chop any larger pieces of vegetable and slice the potatoes. Place in a bowl and

When travelling, try to take with you the child's usual bedding. A familiar pillow is especially conducive to a good night's sleep. This also works wonders for adults, in an otherwise unfamiliar motel environment.

A fat baby is not a healthy baby. This unfortunate myth is finally being well and truly dispelled by the latest research in nutrition. Fat babies often become fat children, depressed and overweight adolescents, and finally obese adults, who need serious counselling or even drastic surgery to overcome their bad eating habits. Educate your child early, and in turn, learn to listen: when your child says 'No', it may be because their stomach is full and they simply don't need any more at the moment.

Encourage children to eat slowly. This not only avoids indigestion, it establishes sensible eating habits for a lifetime. Saliva contains enzymes that begin breaking down foods in your mouth, so chewing your food properly is an essential part of the digestive process.

mix with eggs and chives. Melt the butter in a frying pan and pour in the vegetable mixture. Cook on moderate heat until the underside is golden, then cut into quarters and turn. Cook the mixture further until the surface is golden and the egg set. Any leftover cooked meat can be chopped and added as well.

Vegetable Pancakes

Pancake Batter:
1 cup plain (all-purpose) flour
1 large fresh egg
1 egg yolk
1¼ cups (315 mL) milk
1 tablespoon melted butter
Vegetable Filling:
4 cups chopped cooked vegetables
1 cup (250 mL) White Sauce (page 48)
½ cup (60 g) grated Cheddar cheese
½ cup (125 mL) cream

Sift the flour into a bowl and make a well in the centre. Break the egg into the well and add the egg yolk and half the milk. Stir, gradually incorporating the flour from the sides. Add the remaining milk and beat well, then add the melted butter. Leave to stand for 1 hour.

Rub an omelette pan or a heavy frying pan with a buttered cloth and heat to moderate. Pour in a large spoonful of the batter — enough to thinly coat the bottom of the pan. Cook until the underside is golden, then lift it on a spatula and turn. Cook the other side lightly, the remove and cover with a clean tea-towel. Cook the remaining pancakes in this way.

Heat the vegetables with the white sauce and most of the cheese, until heated through. Mix the remaining cheese with the cream.

Place a spoonful of the vegetable mixture in the centre of each pancake and roll up. Arrange in a greased casserole and pour on the cheese and cream mixture. Bake in a preheated hot oven 230°C (450°F/Gas 8) for about 15 minutes. Serve hot.

Filled pancakes can be frozen for later use. After filling, place the pancakes in a plastic freezer box which has been lightly coated with cornflour (cornstarch). Frozen pancakes can go straight into the oven to cook for about 30 minutes.

Potatoes Baked with Tomato and Garlic

500 g cooked potatoes
1–2 cloves garlic, crushed
2 tablespoons butter
500 g tomatoes
½ teaspoon ground oregano or thyme
1½ cups (375 mL) cream
2 teaspoons chopped parsley

Grease an oven dish with butter. Slice the potatoes and layer half in the dish. Sprinkle on half the garlic. Dot with butter. Slice the tomatoes and layer half over the potatoes and sprinkle on half the oregano. Repeat a layer of potato, garlic and seasoning, dot with remaining butter, then add another layer of tomato, and seasoning.

Pour on the cream and place the dish in a modern oven 180°C (350°F/Gas 4). Bake for about 45 minutes, sprinkle on the parsley and serve.

A smaller casserole can be prepared for the young child, omitting the herbs and garlic. This cooks in about 30 minutes.

● As an alternative, replace the tomato with thin slices of lightly sautéed onion and mixed herbs.

Cheesy Vegetable Bake

4 slices bacon
3 large potatoes
3 medium carrots
2 large spring onions
3 tablespoons butter
1 cup (125 g) grated Cheddar cheese

Grill the bacon until very crisp, then remove the rind and chop bacon finely. Peel and slice the potatoes and carrots and shred the spring onions, including most of the green tops.

Brush a sheet of aluminium foil with butter or bacon fat and arrange the potato overlapped on it. Cover the potato layer with the carrots, then scatter on the spring onions, and the butter cut into cubes. Lift the corners of the foil and pull up into the centre, pinch together to enclose the vegetables. Wrap in another piece of foil. Bake in a moderate oven 180°C (350°F/Gas 4) for 1 hour. Open the package, add the crumbled bacon and cheese, close

Fish Mornay (page 62), Bubble and Squeak (page 55) and Vegetable Pancakes (page 56)

and bake a further 6–7 minutes until the cheese is melted.

This could also be cooked in a casserole, covered, until the vegetables are tender. Then remove the lid, add the bacon and cheese and cook on higher heat until the cheese melts.

Baked Chicken and Rice-filled Tomato Cases

4 medium tomatoes
1 small spring onion
¼ cup cooked rice
60 g cooked chicken
1 tablespoon butter, melted
1 tablespoon dry breadcrumbs

Cut tops off the tomatoes and discard. Carefully scoop out the seeds and ribs without damaging the cases. Discard the seeds and chop the remaining tomato pulp. Mince or finely chop the spring onion and chicken and mix with the tomato and rice. Mix half of the butter into the mixture.

Spoon into the tomato cases and place on an oven tray or in a casserole. Coat the tops thickly with breadcrumbs and drizzle on the remaining butter. Bake in a moderate oven 180°C (350°F/Gas 4) for about 20 minutes.

Salads

Fresh salads are as tempting to look at as they are delicious to eat. Children usually enjoy the crisp texture and fresh flavours and should be encouraged to eat salads often, as they are rich in vitamins and essential minerals. Dressings should be kept simple. Mayonnaise, oil and lemon juice, whipped cream cheese or yoghurt will all make tasty dressings for salads. Your child may prefer salads without dressing. The combinations of ingredients to use in your salads will be limited only by your imagination. Here are some suggestions:

• Combine grated cheese, shredded lettuce, chopped apple (sprinkled with lemon juice to prevent discoloration) and a few raisins or sultanas. Mix equal quantities of sour cream and fresh cream to make the dressing.

• Mixed diced apple, chopped celery and raisins or sultanas. Dress with a mixture of mayonnaise and sour cream.

• Slice hard-boiled eggs, peeled or unpeeled cucumber, tomato and onion (optional) and arrange on a bed of alfalfa sprouts. Sprinkle on fresh lemon juice, a dash of sugar, salt and olive oil.

• Arrange quartered hard-boiled eggs on a lettuce leaf and top with slices of avocado. Dress with mayonnaise and a fine dusting of paprika or slivers of green olive.

• Soak 2 slices of wholemeal bread or a piece of pita bread in milk until soft. Squeeze out the milk and break the bread into pieces. Toss in a bowl with chopped tomato and onion and plenty of finely chopped fresh parsley. Drizzle on olive oil and add wedges of lemon.

• Boil macaroni or pasta shells until tender. Drain well and mix with cooked peas, chopped chives or parsley, finely chopped tomato and chopped cooked chicken, ham or turkey. Toss vigorously with salad cream or mayonnaise.

• Cut cooked potatoes or sweet potatoes into cubes and toss with finely chopped chives, parsley or mint, spring onion and sour cream. Add a pinch of curry powder for extra flavour.

• Peel and slice several raw mushrooms and an avocado. Arrange on a lettuce leaf and dress with a mixture of olive oil, fresh lemon juice, chopped parsley, salt, sugar and a little crushed garlic, shaken together in a screw-top jar.

• Mix a variety of cooked dried beans with sliced boiled green beans, a little chopped onion and red or green capsicum (pepper) and dress with mayonnaise or oil and vinegar.

• Trickle mayonnaise over flaked tuna and dot with finely chopped spring onions or chives. Arrange on a bed of julienne (matchstick) vegetables including carrot, cucumber and celery, then garnish with sieved hard-boiled egg yolk.

• Combine strips of cooked meat (roast beef, pork or lamb, chicken or turkey) with chopped celery, cucumber, tomato, avocado, capsicum (red or green pepper) and spring onion (scallions). Dress generously with salad cream, mayonnaise or French dressing.

If going out for the day, make a checklist of essentials: nappies, wash cloth, plastic bag or used nappies, bottles/teats, dummy (pacifier), spare clothes for mini disasters and your child's favourite 'friend' — scrap of blanket, teddy, old sock or whatever.

Cottage Cheese, Fruit and Salad Platter

Press 1 cup (125 g) of creamed cottage cheese into a small dish, then upturn into the centre of a serving plate. Surround with peeled sliced fruit and salad vegetables such as pawpaw, pineapple, melon, avocado, banana, capsicum, apple, celery, radish, cucumber, seedless grapes.

Raw Vegetables with Sour Cream/Yoghurt Dip

Mix 1–1½ cups (250–375 mL) of sour cream or plain yoghurt with ¼ teaspoon dill tips or seeds, a pinch of sugar and 2 tablespoons thickened cream. Pour into a small dish and set in the centre of a serving platter. Surround with peeled, sliced raw vegetables such as cauliflower, broccoli, spring onions, mushrooms, celery, zucchini, cucumber, capsicum, carrot.
• An alternative dip can be prepared with cottage or ricotta cheese. Place in a blender or food processor with a little milk and add chopped chives or dill, a touch of crushed garlic, salt and pepper. Blend until smooth and creamy.

Some vegetables will be extra crisp if prepared in advance and stored in a glass of iced water in the refrigerator. This applies to celery, cucumber, zucchini and carrot. Other vegetables may soften if left in water.

Fish and Seafood

The moist method of cooking used in *Fish and Mushrooms*, which is rather like a stroganoff, keeps the fish tender.

Fish and Mushrooms

15 g butter
1 medium onion, finely sliced
1 cup button mushrooms, thinly sliced
¾ cup cream
2 tablespoons finely chopped parsley
1 tablespoon lemon juice
2 teaspoons finely grated lemon rind
500 g boneless white fish fillets
1 cup coarse breadcrumbs
15 g butter, extra

1 Heat butter in pan. Add onion and cook until soft. Add mushrooms, cream, parsley, lemon juice, and lemon rind.

Seafood Rice (page 72)

Lullabies are universal favourites with both parents and children. They contain comforting words and when sung to a rocking motion, lull even the most restless babies to sleep. 'Hush-a-bye-baby' is one of the oldest lullabies and refers to the ancient custom of hanging babies in rush baskets in the branches of trees, so the babies were rocked to sleep by gentle winds.

HUSH-A-BYE BABY
Hush-a-bye, baby, on the tree top, When the wind blows, the cradle will rock; When the bough breaks, the cradle will fall, Down will come baby, bough, cradle and all.

2 Place fillets in sauce. Gently simmer until flesh flakes about 5–7 minutes.
3 Place fish and mushroom mixture in an ovenproof dish. Sprinkle breadcrumbs on top. Dot with butter and put under grill or in oven to brown. Serve immediately.

Smoked Haddock Pie

butter
6 slices white bread
500 g smoked haddock (cod)
$^1/_3$ cup (75 mL) milk
1 egg, beaten
2 teaspoons chopped parsley
$^1/_3$ teaspoon finely chopped lemon rind
pinch of white pepper

Thickly butter the bread and cut into fingers. Use a little more than half of the bread fingers to line a suitable pie dish, buttered sides downwards. Flake the smoked fish and mix with the milk, beaten egg, parsley, lemon rind and pepper. Pour in the pie dish. Top with the remaining bread, buttered sides upwards and bake in a preheated moderate oven 180°C (350°F/Gas 4) for about 35 minutes until the top is crisp.

New England style Fish Chowder

4–5 slices streaky bacon (fat bacon)
1 large onion
2 large potatoes
500 g white fish
2 cups (500 mL) milk
1 tablespoon butter

Fry the bacon in a pan until crisp, then remove the rind and cut the bacon into tiny pieces. Coarsely chop the onion and fry in the bacon fat until soft. Peel and cube the potatoes then boil in lightly salted water for 5–6 minutes. Add the fried onions (the bacon fat can be strained off first, if preferred) and boil for a further 5–6 minutes, then add the fish cut into cubes and reduced heat to low. Simmer for about 5 minutes, then add the milk and heat almost to boiling. Leave to cool to allow time for the flavours to seep into the milk, then reheat, add the butter, and stir the chopped bacon into the chowder.

Fish Pie

4 fillets fish (approx. 410 g)
1 medium onion
2 medium tomatoes
2 tablespoons butter
2 teaspoons chopped parsley
piece of bay leaf
milk or water to cover
cornflour
Topping:
3 large potatoes, boiled
milk or butter
2 tablespoons grated cheese
1½ tablespoons dry breadcrumbs

Cut the fish into cubes. Finely chop the onion and tomatoes and sauté in the butter until softened. Add the fish, parsley, bay leaf and just enough milk or water to cover. Simmer gently until the fish is tender. Thicken the liquid with a mixture of cornflour and cold water, stirring until the sauce clears. Transfer to a pie dish. Mash potatoes with a little milk or butter. Spread over the fish. Mix the cheese and breadcrumbs together and cover the potatoes. Dot with butter and bake in a hot oven 230° (450°F/Gas 8) for about 10 minutes, until the top is golden.

Fish Baked in Foil with Herb Butter

4 fillets fish (approx. 410 g)
2 tablespoons softened butter
1 tablespoon lemon juice
1 tablespoon chopped fresh herbs (dill, chives, parsley, chervil, basil, thyme)
2 teaspoons vegetable oil

Cut four pieces of heavy aluminium foil or a double thickness of regular foil, each large enough to wrap one piece of fish.

Mix the softened butter with the lemon juice, herbs and oil and spread some in the centre of each piece of foil. Place a fillet of fish in each and spread on the remaining butter. Wrap each of the packages, sealing at the top. Place on a baking tray, bake in a preheated oven 230°C (450°F/Gas 8) about 15 minutes.

Sautéed or creamed spinach and boiled new potatoes with a dressing of yoghurt or sour cream and chopped chives make excellent accompaniments to this dish.

New England Chowder (opposite), Mini Chicken Drumsticks (page 63) and Lamb Kebabs (page 65)   61

Fish Mornay

4 fillets white fish (approx. 410 g)
1 medium onion
2 tablespoons butter
1½ cups (375 mL) milk
1½ tablespoons plain (all-purpose) flour
¼ teaspoon mustard powder (optional)
2-3 teaspoons lemon juice
2 teaspoons chopped parsley
2 tablespoons grated Cheddar cheese

Cut the fish into cubes. Finely chop the onion and sauté in 1 tablespoon of the butter until softened. Add the fish and saute briefly, then add the milk and bring to the boil. Simmer for 2 minutes; then remove from the heat.

In another saucepan melt the remaining butter and add the flour. Stir for 1 minute, then strain in the milk from the fish and stir on moderate heat until the sauce thickens and cooks.

Add mustard powder, if using it, lemon juice, parsley and 1 tablespoon cheese.

Transfer the fish to a greased casserole and pour on the sauce. Scatter the remaining cheese on the top and bake in a preheated hot oven 230°C (450°F/Gas 8) for about 10 minutes.

When giving chicken to small children, remove the small bones and cartilage from the wings and the fine splinter bones from drumsticks.

Chinese-style Steamed Fish on Vegetables

4 fillets fish (approx. 410 g)
1 medium carrot
½ stick celery
1 small spring onion
4 fresh mushrooms
2 teaspoons light soy sauce
2 teaspoons vegetable oil

Choose fillets with the skin on. Cut the vegetables into julienne strips and place on a dish which will fit into a steamer. Arrange the fish, skin side upwards, on the vegetables. Mix the soy sauce and vegetable oil together, pour over the fish. Place the fish in steamer, cover, steam over gently boiling water for about 10 minutes.

To cook this dish in the oven, arrange the ingredients, as above, in an oven dish and add ¼–½ cup (60–125 mL) of water. Cover. Bake in moderate oven 180°C (350°F/Gas 4) for about 20 minutes.

Chicken

Chicken Breasts Florentine

3 half chicken breasts
(approx. 625 g)
1½ tablespoons butter
500 g fresh or frozen spinach
Sauce:
1 tablespoon butter
2 tablespoons plain (all-purpose) flour
1 cup (250 mL) chicken stock
¾ cup (185 mL) cream
½ cup (60 g) grated cheese
pinch of mustard (optional)

Remove skin and bone from the breasts and cut each in halves. Sauté in the butter until almost cooked through, about 2 minutes on each side. Thaw the spinach if frozen, or chop well-washed fresh spinach, and spread it in a well-greased oven dish. Arrange the chicken breasts on top of the spinach.

Melt the butter in a saucepan and add the flour. Stir for 1 minute, then add the chicken stock and bring to the boil, stirring constantly. Simmer for about 5 minutes, then stir in the cream, most of the cheese, and the mustard, if you are using it. Pour the sauce over the chicken. Cover with the remaining cheese and bake in a preheated hot oven 230°C (450°F/ Gas 8) for about 12 minutes.

Baked Chicken Wings

12 chicken wings
1 tablespoon light soy sauce
1 tablespoon vegetable oil
2 teaspoons dry sherry
¾ teaspoon grated fresh ginger
½ teaspoon Chinese five-spice powder or crushed garlic

Use only the end two joins of the wings, reserving the shoulder joins for the following, or another, recipe. Place wings in lightly oiled oven dish and add the remaining ingredients, mixed together. Cover with plastic wrap and leave for 1 hour, turning once or twice. Remove plastic and bake in a preheated moderate oven 180°C (350°F/Gas 4) for 25–30 minutes.

Mini Drumsticks

*12 chicken wings (reserved from the
previous recipe)
cornflour (cornstarch)
2 egg whites, beaten
1½ cups (185 g) dry breadcrumbs
deep frying oil*

Use a small sharp knife to separate the meat from the bones at the meaty end of each wing bone. Push the meat along the bone and fold it over the end of the bone to form a ball shape. Coat each piece lightly with cornflour. Dip the floured chicken into the beaten egg whites and coat with breadcrumbs.

Heat the deep frying oil and fry the mini-drumsticks several at a time until golden, about 2½ minutes each. Drain and serve with tomato mayonnaise or a soy sauce dip.

● To make tomato mayonnaise: mix equal parts of tomato sauce and mayonnaise and add a pinch of finely chopped dill or parsley and a little crushed garlic or chopped onion.

Chicken and Bacon Casserole

*3 whole chicken thighs or approx. 625 g
chicken pieces
2 large tomatoes
1 medium onion
1 medium carrot
3 rashers bacon
¼ teaspoon dried mixed herbs or a piece
of bay leaf
1 teaspoon chicken stock powder*

Cut the thighs through at the central joint. Place in a lightly greased casserole. Cut the peeled tomatoes and onion into wedges. Peel the carrot and cut into cubes. Add the vegetables to the casserole. Remove rind from the bacon, cut each piece in half and place over the vegetables. Fill the casserole with enough water to just cover the ingredients, then add the herbs and stock powder. Cover and place in a moderate oven 180°C (350°F/Gas 4). Cook for 2 hours. The sauce can be thickened, if preferred, using cornflour (cornstarch) mixed to a paste with cold water.

Serve the chicken with some of the pan liquid, or reserve the liquid to make a soup. A simple and nourishing soup can be made by drizzling in 2–3 beaten eggs and adding chopped parsley. Do not stir the soup until the egg has set.

Chicken Cordon Bleu

*2 whole chicken breasts (approx. 750 g)
2 thin slices cooked ham
¾ cup (90 g) grated Cheddar cheese
flour
2 eggs, beaten
1½ cups (185 g) dry breadcrumbs
½ cup (125 mL) vegetable oil
2 tablespoons butter*

Remove skin and bone from the breasts and cut each in half along the central bone. Make a slit in each piece, cutting almost through. Fold open, then place on a worktop between two pieces of grease-proof paper. Flatten by gently pounding with a rolling pin.

Cut the ham into pieces half the size of the chicken, and place one piece on each piece of chicken. Cover with a portion of the grated cheese and fold in half, pinching the edges of the chicken together, to completely encase the ham and cheese.

Coat the chicken with the four, then brush each piece with the beaten egg and coat with breadcrumbs.

Heat the vegetable oil and butter together in a large pan. Fry the chicken, two pieces at a time, until cooked through, about 2 minutes on each side. Drain and serve at once.

● Children may prefer plain chicken fried in crumbs. Proceed as above, pounding the chicken into thin pieces, then coat with flour, egg and crumbs. They should cook in about 1½ minutes on each side. Dip a peeled banana into egg and crumbs and fry for about 2½ minutes to serve as an accompaniment.

Meat

Beef Stroganoff

750 g beef fillet
90 g butter
1 medium onion
500 g fresh mushrooms, sliced thinly
½ cup (125 mL) beef stock
1 × 315 g can tomatoes
1¼ (315 mL) cups sour cream
1 teaspoon cornflour

Trim the meat and cut into thin slices, then into strips. Melt half the butter in a large frying pan and sauté the meat in several lots until lightly coloured. Remove. Add the remaining butter as needed. Finely chop the onion and sauté in the butter, then add the mushrooms and sauté for 3 minutes. Return the meat to the pan and add the beef stock. Chop the tomatoes and add to the meat with the liquid from the can. Bring just to the boil, then reduce the heat and simmer for about 6 minutes. Stir in the sour cream mixed with the cornflour and simmer 5 minutes.

Serve on boiled noodles moistened with butter and flavoured with finely chopped parsley or other fresh herbs.

Pot Roast of Beef

750 g topside
1 tablespoon plain (all-purpose) flour
pepper
1 tablespoon butter
1 large onion
2 medium tomatoes
1 medium carrot
2 teaspoons chopped parsley
1 bay leaf
2 teaspoons tomato paste
¾ cup (185 mL) beef stock or water
1-2 tablespoons sour or thickened cream

Trim the meat. Mix the flour and pepper together and rub into the meat. Heat the butter in a large pan and brown the meat on all surfaces. Finely chop the onion, tomatoes and carrot. Add to the pan and sauté for a short time, then add the parsley, bay leaf and tomato paste with the beef stock or water. Cover the pan tightly and bake in a slow oven 150°C (300°F/Gas 2) for 2–2½ hours.

Turn the meat several times during cooking, and baste with the pan ingredients. Stir the sour or thickened cream into the gravy before serving.

Scotch Egg Loaf

625 g pork sausage meat, or very finely minced lean pork
625 g lean minced beef
2 eggs
2 medium onions
1 tablespoon chopped parsley
1 clove garlic
5 hard-boiled eggs
2 tablespoons dry breadcrumbs
1 tablespoon butter

Place the sausage meat and minced beef in a mixing bowl and add the raw eggs, the onion, very finely chopped, and the parsley. Crush the garlic and add it to the meat. Mix these together thoroughly.

Spread half the mixture in a greased loaf tin. Peel the hard-boiled eggs and place end to end along the centre of the meat mixture. Cover with the remaining meat, pressing down firmly to ensure that the eggs are completely encased. Cover the top with crumbs and dot with butter. Bake in a moderately hot oven 220°C (425°F/Gas 7) for 1 hour.

Unmould and slice before serving.

Serve hot with a rich brown gravy or home-made tomato sauce or serve cold with tomato mayonnaise (see *Mini Drumsticks* page 63) or pickles.

Meatballs in Yoghurt Sauce

625 g lean minced beef
1 small onion
1 tablespoon chopped parsley
¼ teaspoon dried marjoram
1 egg
1 tablespoon dry breadcrumbs
1½ cups (375 mL) plain yoghurt
2 teaspoons cornflour

Place beef in a mixing bowl. Finely chop the onion and add to meat with the parsley, marjoram, egg and breadcrumbs. Mix thoroughly, then use wet hands to form the mixture into small balls.

Place in a greased oven dish. Mix the cornflour into the yoghurt and pour the

NEVER leave a baby or toddler in the bath, shower or kitchen sink alone. If the phone rings, either ignore it or wrap the child in a warm towel and take her or him with you. It takes 1 teaspoon of water in the lungs to kill an adult, much less a tiny baby, and drowning is a very quiet death.

mixture over the meatballs. Bake in a moderate oven 180°C (350°F/Gas 4) for 25 minutes.

The meatballs can be shallow fried in a mixture of vegetable oil and butter, deep fried in vegetable oil or steamed, or they can be baked with the yoghurt.

The fried meatballs can be threaded onto bamboo skewers or toothpicks and served with the yoghurt, hot or cold, as a dip. To heat the yoghurt, add the cornflour and bring almost to the boil. If serving cold, do not add the cornflour.
● Mix finely grated cucumber and chopped mint into the yoghurt for extra flavour.

Lamb Kebabs

750 g lean lamb
¾ cup (185 mL) plain yoghurt
2 teaspoons lemon juice
melted butter

Trim the lamb and cut it into cubes. Place it in a dish and add the yoghurt and lemon juice and leave for 1½ hours. Thread onto bamboo or metal skewers. Brush with melted butter and cook under a moderate grill (broiler) for about 15 minutes until the meat is tender. Brush with butter and any remaining marinade during cooking.

Remove the meat from the skewers before serving to toddlers.

Pat-a-cake, pat-a-cake, baker's man,
Make me a cake as fast as you can;
Pat it and prick it, and mark it with B,
And toss it in the oven for baby and me.

Scotch Egg Loaf

Apple Cup Cakes (page 74), Zucchini Boats (page 55) and Beef Stroganoff with noodles (page 64)

Eggs

Fried Eggs

A quick and nourishing snack. Add interest by cooking in an edible casing:
• a ring of red or green capsicum (fry it briefly in butter before adding the egg),
• a square slice of bread with a round section removed from the centre (fry in butter on one side, then invert and add the egg),
• fry an egg on top of a thick slice of tomato.

Bacon and Egg (single serve)

Grill half a rasher of bacon until crisp, remove rind and chop the bacon finely or crumble. Break an egg onto the bacon fat and fry until soft cooked, sprinkling the bacon bits over the top.

Tomato Scramble

Scramble an egg with a little milk or water in 1 teaspoon of butter. Hollow out a large tomato, warm it through in the frying pan and then fill it with the egg.

Bacon Scramble

Crumble crisp bacon into a beaten egg. Add 1 tablespoon of milk and cook in the top of a double saucepan until firm, or scramble in a pan with a little butter.

Soufflé Omelette

For one serving, beat 1 egg with 2 teaspoons of water and a pinch of cornflour (cornstarch). Beat the white of another egg to soft peaks and carefully fold into the first egg mixture. Melt 2 teaspoons butter in an omelette pan and pour in the egg. Cook until well risen and lightly coloured underneath. Then cook the top by placing under a moderate grill.

Prepare fillings of spinach purée or creamed spinach, tuna or flaked smoked fish, grated cheese, sautéed tomato with onions and cheese, sautéed mushrooms or leftover vegetables in *White Sauce* (page 48). Place filling along the centre of the omelette. Fold one side over to encase filling and cook until warmed through and the egg is just firm.

Soup

Vegetable Soup

2 medium carrots
1 stalk celery
2 medium potatoes
½ cup frozen peas
1 medium onion
2 medium tomatoes
4–5 cabbage leaves, chopped
5 cups (1.25 litres) chicken stock or beef tea
¾ cup (125 g) small pasta shapes or broken spaghetti
slices of toast
½ cup (60 g) grated cheese

Slice the carrots, celery, potatoes, onion and tomatoes. Fry the vegetables in a mixture of butter and vegetable oil for 2–3 minutes, then add the stock and pasta and simmer for about 20 minutes. Spread several slices of toasted bread with butter, cut into squares. Cover with cheese and place under a hot grill. Float these on the soup just before serving.

Tomato Soup

8 medium tomatoes, skinned
butter
1 cup finely chopped celery, onion and carrot
3 cups (750 mL) chicken stock
1 teaspoon sugar
1 sprig parsley
1 bay leaf
1 cup (250 mL) milk
1¼ tablespoons cornflour
2 teaspoons chopped parsley
toast to serve

Chop the tomatoes and sauté in a little butter for 3–4 minutes. Set aside. Sauté the chopped vegetables in a little more butter then add the stock and seasonings and bring to the boil. Simmer for 10 minutes, then purée in a blender. Return to the saucepan and add the tomatoes. Simmer until completely tender, then pass through a sieve to remove any seeds.

Mix the milk and cornflour together and slowly stir into the soup, heat until thickened, stirring continuously. Garnish with chopped parsley, serve with toast.

Ride a cock-horse to Banbury Cross,
To see a fine lady upon a white horse;
With rings on her fingers and bells on her toes,
She shall have music wherever she goes.

Chicken Cream Corn Soup

125 g boneless chicken
125 g canned sweet corn kernels
3 cups (750 mL) chicken stock
1 spring onion, chopped
2¾ tablespoons cornflour
2 tablespoons milk
1–2 eggs, beaten

Cut the chicken into small dice. Crush the corn in a food processor or blender, but do not purée. Bring the chicken stock to the boil and add the chicken, corn, spring onion and the cornflour mixed with a little cold water. Simmer for 5 minutes. Remove from the heat and add the milk, then slowly pour in the egg in a thin stream. Leave without stirring until the egg sets in strands in the hot soup.

Tomato Soup (page 67)
and toast triangles

Scotch Broth

500 g lamb neck chops
2 medium carrots
1 small turnip
1 medium onion
2 tomatoes
1 small clove garlic
1 teaspoon chopped parsley
60 g soaked pearl barley
pinch of thyme

Brown the neck chops in a little butter then transfer to a large saucepan. Dice all vegetables and sauté briefly in butter than add to the chops with water to cover — or use beef tea. Add the garlic, parsley, barley and thyme and bring to the boil. Simmer, covered, for 1¼–1½ hours until the meat is completely tender. Scrape the meat from the bones before serving.

Chicken Meatballs in Soup

375 g boneless chicken
1 spring onion
cornflour
3½ cups (875 mL) chicken stock
1½ tablespoons frozen peas
1½ tablespoons finely diced carrot
1 tablespoon alphabet noodles or broken spaghetti

Finely mince the chicken. Mince half the spring onion and slice the remainder. Add the minced spring onion to the chicken and mix in thoroughly, then form the mixture into small balls, adding a little cornflour. Bring the chicken stock to the boil and add peas, carrot and noodles. Simmer until the vegetables are tender, then add the sliced spring onion.

Take a handful of the chicken mixture and squeeze a stream of it out between curled forefinger and thumb. Scoop it off with a spoon — it should be about the size of a walnut — and drop into the simmering soup. Repeat until all the chicken has been used. Cook until the meatballs float and turn white. Serve.

Alternatively, the chicken can be cut into thin slices, then coated lightly with cornflour, placed between two sheets of greaseproof paper and gently pounded with a rolling pin to make almost transparent slices. These will cook in seconds in the hot soup.

Quick Meals and Snacks

There are times when you're just not hungry enough for a full meal, but don't want to settle for something out of a can or from a take-away restaurant. These recipes can be made in minutes and are nourishing and economical.

Ham and Cheese Croissants (or Muffins)

Slit open 6 stale croissants and arrange the bottom pieces on a baking tray. Shred 4 slices of ham and 1 spring onion (scallion) and sauté lightly in a little butter. Prepare 1 cup of white sauce and add 2–3 tablespoons of grated cheese. When the cheese has melted add the ham and heat through. Spoon the mixture over the croissants, put the tops in place and heat through in a very hot oven 240°C (475°F/ Gas 9) for 5–6 minutes.

For younger children, chop the ham finely and mix with *White Sauce* (page 48) and a little cheese. Spoon over half a croissant and serve. Day-old muffins can also be used up in this way.

Instant Pizzas

Split 3 muffins in halves and spread lightly with butter or olive oil. Chop the tomatoes from a 375 g can after draining away the liquid (use it in a soup). Spread tomato over the muffins and top with strips of cooked ham, bacon or chicken, then cover with grated cheese. Garnish adults' and older children's servings with smoked oysters, anchovy or olives. Bake in a pre-heated hot oven 240°C (475°F/Gas 9) until well warmed and the cheese melted.

The small sized Pitta breads can be used instead of muffins.

Burger Kings

4 frozen beef burgers
2 rashers bacon
1 medium onion
4 eggs
4 hamburger buns
¾ cup finely shredded lettuce
½ cup (60 g) grated soft cheese
relish or tomato sauce

Thaw the burgers and grill until cooked. Grill the bacon until crisp, remove rind then chop. Thinly slice the onion, separate into rings, cook on the grill. Fry the eggs.

Cut all of the hamburger buns in half, and place on a baking tray. Lightly toast all pieces under the grill.

Butter thinly. Arrange onion over buns, top with beef burgers and cook under a moderate grill for a few minutes to warm through. Cover with bacon and top evenly with grated cheese, then grill until the cheese melts. Top with fried eggs, add shredded lettuce, relish or tomato sauce if desired, and serve.

For young children, do not assemble the hamburger, but serve the various components, buttered bun, beef burger, shredded lettuce, grated cheese and fried egg, separately.

Pitta Roll-ups

Butter pieces of Pitta bread. Fill each with a layer of finely shredded lettuce, grated cheese and shredded ham. Roll up tightly and secure at 5 cm intervals with toothpicks. Cut between the toothpicks into serving pieces.
● A variety of fillings can be used in this way: sautéed minced beef; grated carrot, raisins and alfalfa sprouts; scrambled egg and lettuce.

'Ring-a-Ring o' Roses' is one of the first acting games toddlers enjoy. Everyone takes hands and walks around in a circle, falling down on the last line of the rhyme.

RING O' ROSES
Ring a ring o' roses,
A pocket full of posies;
Hush! Hush! Hush!
And we all tumble down.

Instant Pizza (this page)

Pasta and Rice

Tuna on Pasta Shells

155 g pasta shells
1 × 220 g can tuna
¾ cup cooked peas
1 tablespoon butter
1½ tablespoons plain (all-purpose) flour
1¾ cups (440 mL) milk
1 cup (125 g) grated soft cheese
2 teaspoons chopped parsley
½ cup (60 g) fresh breadcrumbs

Cook the pasta in boiling water with a little olive or vegetable oil added to prevent the pieces sticking together. Drain and transfer to a greased oven dish. Flake the tuna and mix into pasta with peas. Melt the butter in a saucepan and add the flour. Cook for 1 minute, then pour in the milk and stir until it thickens and cooks, about 4 minutes. Stir in half the grated cheese and add the parsley. Pour over the tuna and pasta and stir in lightly.

Mix the remaining cheese with the breadcrumbs, spread over the sauce and dot with butter. Bake in a preheated hot oven 230°C (450°F/Gas 8) for about 15 minutes.

Add canned tomato, chopped, for extra flavour and colour. Substitute cooked white or smoked fish for the tuna, or use canned salmon.

Herb Rice

1 cup (185 g) short grain rice
1¾ cups (440 mL) water
1 teaspoon dried mixed herbs
1 teaspoon chopped parsley
2 teaspoons butter

Wash the rice and place in a saucepan with the water. Add the herbs, cover and bring to the boil. Reduce the heat and simmer gently for about 20 minutes until the rice is tender and fluffy. Stir in the chopped parsley and butter.

Macaroni with Beef and Tomato Sauce

185 g macaroni
375 g lean minced beef
1 medium onion
2½ tablespoons butter
1 × 375 g can tomatoes
¾ cup (185 mL) tomato juice
¾ teaspoon dried basil
1 teaspoon sugar
1 tablespoon plain (all-purpose) flour
½ cup (60 g) dry breadcrumbs
½ cup (60 g) grated soft cheese

Boil the macaroni in a large saucepan of water until just tender, then drain and transfer the macaroni to a buttered oven dish. Sauté the minced beef and finely chopped onion in half of the butter until the meat changes colour. Chop the tomatoes and add to the meat with the liquid from the can, the tomato juice, basil and sugar. Cover and simmer for 15 minutes. Mix the flour with the remaining butter and stir into the meat. Cook gently until the mixture thickens. Pour over the macaroni. Mix the breadcrumbs and cheese together and spread over the top. Bake in a preheated hot oven 240°C (475°C/Gas 9) until the top is crisp, about 12 minutes.

Steamed Chicken Meatballs on Rice

315 g boneless chicken
3 spring onions
1½ cups (280 g) short grain rice
1½ teaspoons chicken stock powder
2¾ cups (660 mL) water

Chop the chicken and 1 spring onion in a food processor or blender until smooth and paste-like. Use wet hands to form into small balls. Place the rice in a saucepan and add the stock powder and water. Bring to the boil, covered, then reduce the heat to very low and simmer for 10 minutes until the water is below the level of the rice. Shred the remaining spring onions and arrange on the rice, then place the meatballs on top. Cover the pan and cook for a further 12 minutes until the rice and meatballs are tender.

Little Bo-peep has lost her sheep,
And can't tell where to find them;
Leave them alone, and they'll come home,
And bring their tails behind them.

Macaroni with Beef and Tomato Sauce, and Steamed Chicken Meatballs on Rice (opposite)

Fruity Rice

Cook short or long grain rice until tender. Sauté ½ cup (60 g) of raisins or sultanas (seedless raisins) in 15 g of butter until lightly coloured. Stir into the rice.

Macaroni in Mushroom Sauce

185 g macaroni (or shell pasta)
375 g fresh mushrooms
125 g butter
2 tablespoons plain (all-purpose) flour
2 cups (500 mL) milk
pinch of mace or nutmeg
2 teaspoons chopped parsley
¾ cup (90 g) fresh breadcrumbs

Cook the macaroni or pasta in a large saucepan of boiling water until tender. Drain the pasta and transfer it to a greased oven dish. Peel and thinly slice the mushrooms and their stems. Sauté in the butter until softened. Remove and spread over the macaroni. Sprinkle the flour into the saucepan over the remaining butter, adding an extra tablespoon if it has been absorbed by the mushrooms. Stir for 1 minute, then add the milk and nutmeg and bring to the boil. Stir on moderate heat until the sauce thickens and cooks, about 5 minutes. Add the parsley, pour over the macaroni and mushrooms, and stir in lightly. Cover with breadcrumbs, dot with a little extra butter and bake in a preheated oven 180°C (350°F/Gas 4) until the top is crisp, about 20 minutes.

Children may not always enjoy wholemeal pastas and brown rice. For young children who do not like fibrous foods very much there is little advantage in forcing the issue.

Seafood Rice

1 cup (185 g) short grain rice
1¾ cups (440 mL) of water
250 g fish (or mixed fish, prawns and scallops)
1 spring onion
2 medium tomatoes
1 teaspoon parsley
lemon juice

Wash the rice and drain thoroughly. Add the water and bring to the boil, covered. Reduce heat to very low and simmer until the water is almost absorbed and the rice almost cooked.

Cut the fish into cubes and arrange over the rice. Dice the spring onions and tomatoes and add to the fish with the parsley and a few teaspoons of lemon juice. Cover again and cook until the rice is completely tender and the fish cooked. Stir the fish and vegetables into the rice and add lemon juice to taste.

Buttered Pea Rice

1 cup (155 g) long grain rice
1¾ cups (440 mL) water
2 tablespoons butter
½ cup frozen peas

Place all ingredients in a heavy saucepan and cover. Bring to the boil and boil briskly for 1 minute, then reduce heat to the lowest point and simmer for 20 minutes until the rice is tender and fluffy and the peas cooked through. Stir once or twice during cooking to evenly distribute the butter and peas.

Vegetable Rice

1 cup (155 g) long grain rice
1¾ cups (440 mL) water
1 cup mixed diced vegetables (carrot, peas, beans, celery, mushrooms)
French dressing

Boil the rice in the water for 1 minute then reduce the heat to very low and simmer for a further 18–20 minutes until the rice is tender. Boil the vegetables (except celery and mushrooms) separately until tender. Drain, add the remaining vegetables, and toss in French dressing. When the rice is ready stir in the vegetables. Serve hot or cold.

Desserts

Baked Raisin Apples

4 cooking apples
1/3 cup (3 oz) brown sugar
1½ tablespoons chopped raisins
½ teaspoon cinnamon (optional)
1½ tablespoons butter

Core the apples and score the skin around the middle. Combine the sugar, raisins and cinnamon, if you are using it. Place each apple on a piece of heavy-duty aluminium foil and stuff it with the filling. Spread a little butter over the top of each apple, wrap the foil securely around the apples and bake in a hot oven 220°C (425°F/Gas 7) or over a barbecue until cooked, about 35 minutes. Serve with whipped cream or ricotta cream.

Ricotta Cream

Whip equal quantities of ricotta cheese and thickened cream together and sweeten with honey or brown sugar. Use as a dip for fresh or canned fruits, as a creamy filling for pastries or in place of whipped cream.

Yoghurt Cream Cheese with Fruit

Blend 2 parts cream cheese with 1 part plain yoghurt. Pour into a wet jelly mould and refrigerate until firm. Turn out onto a glass platter and surround with washed fresh fruit.

This can be served as a starter or a dessert.

Yoghurt Sherbet

2 cups (500 mL) plain yoghurt
2 cups (315 g) fresh fruit, diced

Freeze the yoghurt until it begins to firm. Transfer to a blender and blend with the fruit. Freeze again. To serve scrape off with a spoon. Serve with sliced fresh or canned fruit.

Blender Fruit Ice-Cream

¾ cup (185 g) thickened cream
3 cups (470 g) fresh or drained canned berries (strawberries, blackberries, blueberries)
¼ cup honey
½ cup (125 mL) fruit juice or liquid from canned berries
juice of 1 lemon

Whip the cream and turn in a serving bowl. Blend the remaining ingredients until smooth, fold into the cream and freeze. Remove and beat thoroughly twice in the blender, refreezing until hard between each beating.

Honey Ice-Cream

¾ cup (280 g) honey
4 eggs, separated
imitation vanilla essence, to taste
2 cups (500 mL) thickened cream

Beat the honey, egg yolks and vanilla essence until very creamy. Fold in the cream and then stiffly beaten egg whites. Freeze. Remove from the freezer and beat thoroughly twice, returning to the freezer each time.

Bread and Butter Pudding

6 slices white bread
3 cups (875 mL) milk
¼ teaspoon grated lemon rind
½ cup (125 g) sugar
4 eggs
¾ cup (125 g) mixed dried fruits
(sultanas [seedless raisins], raisins, chopped apricots, currants, mixed peel)

Thickly butter the bread and remove the crusts. Heat the milk in a saucepan and add the lemon rind. Bring to the boil, then cover and remove from the heat, leaving to infuse for 10 minutes. Beat the sugar and eggs together, strain the milk over the eggs and mix well.

Scatter half the dried fruit over the bottom of a greased oven dish and arrange the bread, buttered sides downwards, on top. Pour in half the custard, then repeat, adding the remaining fruit, bread and custard. Place the dish in a bain marie and cook in a moderate oven 180°C (350°F/Gas 4) for 35 minutes.

Old King Cole
Was a merry old soul,
And a merry old soul
was he;
He called for his pipe,
And he called for his bowl,
And he called for his
fiddlers three.

73

*Baked Raisin Apples,
Blender Fruit Ice-Cream,
and Bread and Butter
Pudding (all on page 73)*

Humpty Dumpty sat
on a wall.
Humpty Dumpty had
a great fall;
All the king's horses
and all the king's men
Couldn't put Humpty
together again.

Apple Cup Cakes

1 cup apple sauce or canned pie apples
90 g butter
¾ cup (125 g) brown sugar
1 tablespoon honey
1 egg
1 cup (125 g) wholemeal self-raising
flour
½ cup (60 g) white self-raising flour
1 teaspoon cinnamon
pinch of powdered cloves

Purée the pie apples. Beat the butter, sugar and honey together until light and creamy, then add the egg and the apple. Sift in the flours and spices and mix well. Spoon into paper patty cups and bake in a moderate oven 180°C (350°F/Gas 4) for about 20 minutes. When cool, coat with whipped cream and decorate with slivers of dried apple. Makes approximately 36.

Banana Bread

60 g butter
½ cup (90 g) brown sugar
1 egg
1 cup (90 g) of a bran cereal
5 ripe bananas, mashed
a few drops imitation vanilla essence
1 cup (125 g) wholemeal plain (all-
purpose) flour
½ cup (6 oz) plain (all-purpose) flour
2 teaspoons baking powder

Cream the butter and sugar and add the egg, then the bran cereal, bananas and vanilla essence. Sift in the flours and the baking powder and mix them together thoroughly.

Pour into a greased loaf tin and bake in a preheated moderate oven 180°C (350°F/Gas 4) for about 1 hour. This tastes delicious served warm or cold.

Biscuits, Muffins and Cakes

Bran Muffins

1 cup (250 mL) milk
2 tablespoons golden syrup (light corn syrup)
1½ teaspoons bicarbonate of soda (baking soda)
1½ cups (140 g) bran cereal
1½ cups (185 g) wholemeal flour
¾ cup (125 g) sultanas (seedless raisins)
1 tablespoon melted butter

Mix the milk and syrup and warm slightly in a mixing bowl. Stir the bicarbonate soda into the warmed mixture and, as soon as it froths, add the bran cereal and flour, then the fruit and the melted butter. Mix thoroughly.

Lightly butter the recesses of a muffin tin and half-fill with the batter. Bake in a preheated moderate oven 180°C (350°F/Gas 4) oven for 20 minutes. Cool in the tin for a few minutes, then remove and cool completely on a cake rack. Store in an airtight container.

Muesli Crunch Biscuits

125 g butter
¾ cup (90 g) brown sugar
a few drops imitation vanilla essence
1 egg
½ cup (60 g) wholemeal self-raising flour
3 cups (400 g) muesli (no nuts)
1 cup (125 g) chopped dried apricots

Cream the butter and sugar together, then add the vanilla essence and egg and beat well. Sift in the flour, add the muesli and stir in the chopped fruit.

Lightly grease several biscuit trays. Shape the mixture into balls and place on the trays, flatten lightly with a fork and bake in a moderately hot oven 190°C (375°F/Gas 5) for 10–12 minutes. Cool on cake racks, then store in an airtight container. Makes approximately 24.

For variety, substitute some of the muesli with cornflakes or bran flakes, and mix the chopped apricots with other dried fruits.

Oatmeal Biscuits

1 cup (125 g) plain (all-purpose) flour
½ teaspoon baking powder
125 g butter
¾ cup (125 g) brown sugar
1 egg
a few drops imitation vanilla essence
1 tablespoon milk
1 cup (90 g) rolled oats

Sift the flour and baking powder together. Cream the butter and sugar and add the egg, vanilla essence and milk. Beat lightly. Add the sifted flour, then the rolled oats. Drop tablespoonfuls of the mixture onto greased biscuit trays allowing space for the biscuits to spread. Bake in a moderately hot oven 190°C (375°F/Gas 5) for 10–12 minutes. Cool.

Carrot Cake

2 cups grated carrot
1 cup (155 g) brown sugar
1½ tablespoons honey
155 g butter, melted
3 eggs, beaten
1½ teaspoons bicarbonate of soda
1 cup (125 g) wholemeal plain (all-purpose) flour
¾ cup (90 g) plain (all-purpose) flour
1¼ teaspoons cinnamon

In a mixing bowl combine the grated carrot, sugar, honey and butter. Add the eggs and mix well. Sift on the soda, flours and cinnamon and mix thoroughly. Pour into 2 greased and floured 23 cm cake tins and bake in a preheated moderately slow oven 160°C (325°F/Gas 3) for 35–40 minutes. Cool and ice with *Cream Cheese Frosting* (see following recipe).

Cream Cheese Frosting

¾ cup (90 g) cream cheese
½ cup (125 g) milk
3 tablespoons butter
1½ cups (250 g) icing sugar
few drops imitation vanilla essence
extra flavour: dried fruit, wheatgerm, sesame seeds, chocolate or carob pieces or chopped apricot bar

In a blender, whip cream cheese with milk and butter, adding icing sugar and vanilla essence. Add extra flavour of your choice.

Wee Willie Winkie ran through the town, Upstairs and downstairs, in his nightgown; Tapping at the window, crying at the lock; 'Are the babes in their beds, for it's now ten o' clock?'

Drinks for Thirsty Kids

Busy children demand refreshing drinks after play and may raid the refrigerator for carbonated ones if you're not on hand with something better. Soft drinks may be easy to serve, but they are full of artificial colourings, flavourings and sugar.

Water is the only thirst quencher. The use of frozen fruit pieces or frozen diluted fruit juice ice blocks may make water more appealing. There are many drinks you can make up in a blender in just a few minutes or have ready in the refrigerator, using natural ingredients like milk, yoghurt and fruit or fruit juices.

Banana Smoothies

Banana smoothies are superb. Pop a whole banana into the blender and add a cup (250 mL) of milk, a teaspoon of honey and a pinch of wheatgerm. Blend until thick and creamy. A couple of ice cubes added before blending gives extra thickness. Enough for two.

Any canned fruit and most fresh fruits can be made into smoothies.

Equally refreshing are drinks made with plain yoghurt. In India such drinks are called *Lassi* and are always served with a meal. They are particularly good if your child has a mild stomach upset.

Lassi

Blend equal parts of plain yoghurt and water or milk and add a drizzle of honey.

Ice-cream Shake

In the blender whip 1 cup (250 mL) of milk with 2 large scoops of ice-cream and an ice cube, until thick and frothy.

Honey Shake

Blend 1 cup (250 mL) of milk with 2 teaspoons honey and 1 scoop of vanilla ice-cream until thick.

Berry Froth

Add equal parts of canned berries, in their liquid, and milk to the blender and pop in an ice cube. Whip to a froth.

Use canned fruits, apricots, peaches or fruit cocktail, for other fruit drinks.

Frozen Yoghurt Froth

Mix ½ cup (125 mL) plain yoghurt and ½ cup (125 mL) frozen fruit salad yoghurt with ¼ cup (60 mL) milk and ¼ cup (70 g) canned or stewed fruit. Whizz in the blender until thick.

Frothy Frozen Orange

In the blender whip 1 cup (250 mL) water, 1 tablespoon dry milk powder and 1 tablespoon frozen concentrated orange juice to a froth.

Mango and Orange Froth

Use half a fresh mango, chopped, 2 cups (500 mL) orange and mango juice and ½ cup (125 mL) plain yoghurt. Place in the blender and whizz until frothy.

Apricot and Orange Whizz

Blend at high speed 1 cup (250 mL) orange juice with 2 tablespoons apricot nectar and 2 ice cubes.

Apricot Yoghurt Whip

Blend 1 cup (250 mL) plain yoghurt with 1 cup (250 mL) apricot nectar and 2 ice cubes until thick and creamy.

Apple and Grape Juice

Both are deliciously refreshing. Buy the sugar-free variety if it is available. Make into a refreshing drink by mixing with soda water.

Blackcurrant Fizz

Mix concentrated blackcurrant syrup with soda, tonic or plain mineral water.

Hot Drinks

Hot drinks are warming and fortifying in cold weather.

Carob Drink

Carob drink can be made instantly by mixing carob powder and full cream milk powder together. Boil milk or water and stir in the mixture until dissolved.

Hot Milk with Honey

Heat a cupful of milk and stir in 1 teaspoon honey.

Hey diddle diddle,
The cat and the fiddle,
The cow jumped over the moon;
The little dog laughed
To see such craft,
And the dish ran away with the spoon.

Clockwise from top: Frothy Frozen Orange, Grape Juice, Banana Smoothie and Berry Froth

THE LUNCH BOX

Starting kindergarten or pre-school is an important step in your child's life.

Activity can be strenuous. Games to play, dances to learn, paintings and puzzles to perfect, and a multitude of other projects to undertake.

Your choice of food for lunch boxes can help to maintain a good level of energy throughout the day.

A Balanced Meal with a Little Something Extra

Lunch boxes should include a protein-rich food; a piece of fresh fruit or vegetable; (remember water is always available in Kindergartens and daycare centres); the *occasional* little surprise.

Variety may not be important to your child. Mine was happy with a rotation of tuna, ham, peanut butter and Vegemite or Marmite sandwiches, which I made on wholemeal bread.

Try popping in something not usually eaten at home. Often in company children will be more inclined to eat foods they don't

usually like, especially if their friends like them. Do avoid making the whole lunch something he may not eat or you will have a hungry and unhappy child later.

You could use crispbread, plain crackers, raisin bread or muffins instead of bread for sandwiches; or make open sandwiches using fillings which will not be spoiled when wrapped.

Cream cheese topped with shredded lettuce or grated carrot, cucumber slices, cold meat, cheese, grated carrot, raisins and alfalfa sprouts are good. Wrap each sandwich individually with plastic wrap.

Omit bread altogether sometimes, sandwiching sliced cold meat with tomato or sliced cucumber, sliced cucumber with cream cheese, or cheese slices with grated carrot. Always keep portions small so they can be easily managed by little fingers.

No Sweets

Many kindergartens and pre-schools wisely discourage sweet foods in the lunch box. When

included, biscuits and cakes may be made using wholemeal flour, fresh or dried fruits and little or no sugar or other sweetener. There are plenty of tasty alternatives which children enjoy.

Sandwiches are Delicious, Filling and Nutritious

Always use a good wholemeal or multigrain bread for the extra nourishment it offers. Your child will soon become used to the slightly coarser texture. Rye bread may also be enjoyed.

Spread lightly with butter or margarine before filling. Wrap sandwiches with different fillings separately in small pieces of plastic wrap or greaseproof paper.

Some suggested fillings:

Eggs

Hard-boiled and mashed with butter, mayonnaise or cream cheese. Chopped hard-boiled mixed with chopped parsley or shredded lettuce. Sliced hard-boiled topped with alfalfa sprouts, tomato or cucumber. Scrambled and topped with crushed bacon.

Cold Meats

Choose from roast chicken, turkey, lamb, pork, beef, liver pâté, corned beef or luncheon meats. Sandwich with salad vegetables. Top with sliced pickle, mayonnaise or relish. Serve with sliced cheese or pineapple.

Salad

Mixed salad sandwiches are tops. Shredded lettuce, sliced tomato, cheese, grated carrot with drizzle of mayonnaise. Alfalfa sprouts and grated carrot with raisins and cream cheese. Sliced tomato and cucumber.

Cheese

Cream cheese, cottage cheese, ricotta cheese or individually wrapped slices of processed cheese are all suitable for sandwiches. Mix with chopped raisins or crumbled crisp bacon bits. Stir in smooth peanut butter. Flavour with finely chopped dried apricots. Serve with salad vegetables or fruit such as pineapple or banana. Use cheese to top sliced cucumber or tomato. Add crushed pineapple, jam or marmalade.

Tuna Fish

Canned tuna fish (or salmon) is a delicious sandwich filling. Flake and mix with mayonnaise or tartare sauce.

Spread over sliced cucumber, pineapple, avocado, tomato.

Popular sandwich spreads include peanut butter, Vegemite or Marmite, cheese spread, fish and other pastes, jam and honey. However, they can be dry in sandwiches which need to be made several hours before meal time. The addition of cheese, shredded lettuce, alfalfa sprouts and cold meats all make sandwiches more interesting, as well as offering better nutritional value.

Pack sandwiches into a paper bag after wrapping in plastic wrap or greaseproof paper or into a plastic lunch box. Make sure your child can open it.

Never pack lunches into plastic bags which would be large enough to slip over a child's head, unless it's well punctured with holes. Use only small lengths of plastic wrap to wrap the sandwiches or other lunch items.

The possibility of death by suffocation inside a plastic bag or by plastic wrap over the face is very real and can be avoided. A severe lecture about the danger is usually respected by even a young child.

Fresh Fruit and Vegetables

A piece of fresh fruit or several sticks of your child's favourite raw vegetables should always be included in the lunch box.

Peel apples and, if necessary, core and quarter. Rub with orange juice to prevent any discoloration and wrap tightly in plastic. Oranges can be peeled and separated into segments, or quartered without peeling. Wrap in plastic to prevent leakage over the rest of the lunch.

Pop in a small banana, or half a banana still in its peel and with the cut end wrapped in a small piece of aluminium foil. Give any fresh stone fruits in season if you know your child can handle skin and stones without danger.

Raw cucumber, celery and carrot sticks are deliciously crunchy. Prepare them the night before and chill thoroughly in iced water. Then drain and wrap tightly in plastic wrap to retain their crunch.

Vegetarianism and Natural Foods

Choosing vegetarianism for your child is a big decision and one which must be approached rationally and responsibly. We have introduced a dietary plan, many hints and family recipes to guide you through the gains, pains and pitfalls of the vegetarian alternative.

Cucumber and Yoghurt Salad (page 89), Tabbouleh (page 89) and Tuna-stuffed Eggs (page 90)

With school lunchboxes, always *ask* children what they would prefer. On alien territory surrounded by strangers, it can be very comforting to have a favourite food, and very upsetting for them to find something in their lunch they hate. Some children thrive on variety, some love to have the same thing every day, some children like minor variations.

It seems that after a painstaking investigation of the subject, experts have now agreed that a baby can be successfully reared on a vegetarian diet.

There are, however, differing degrees of vegetarianism. The Vegan diet allows only the consumption of plant foods. Such a diet can be nutritionally inadequate, especially during pregnancy and early childhood. The bulky, high fibre and high water content of the Vegan diet can make it difficult for the young, rapidly-growing child to eat enough to satisfy their need for protein and energy (kilojoules/calories). With careful planning, adequate protein and energy can be supplied via legumes (pulses), nuts (use only smooth nut butters and finely-ground nut meal for children less than seven years old), soy products and grains (cereals).

Special care is also needed to ensure adequate intakes of the essential minerals calcium, iron and zinc. The amounts of vitamins supplied by a vegetarian diet are generally adequate except for vitamin B12 which, since it is found almost exclusively in animal products, is often insufficient in Vegan diets. A vitamin B12 supplement or soy milk supplemented with B12 is recommended during pregnancy and breastfeeding when demand for the vitamin is high.

Up to the age of six months, babies will receive all the nourishment they need from breast milk. Special soya-based formulae are available for children under one.

Lacto-vegetarianism, a diet which encompasses plant foods, milk and milk products, can be acceptable to the baby and small child if cautiously and sensibly administered. This too will need special attention to iron and zinc.

A further category of vegetarianism, Lacto-ovo, is by far the most suitable, allowing as it does plant foods, milk and milk products and eggs. This diet can provide adequate protein and the volume of fibre is not excessive.

Add to this diet fish (Pesco-vegetarianism) and you have a range of health-giving natural foods to choose from, which should allow for complete nourishment of any child.

Milk is a Must

Up to the age of one year, a child requires four times the protein of an adult, weight for weight. The mother who plans to rear a vegetarian child should breast feed for as long as possible, at least six months while ensuring that her own diet is well-chosen and supplemented where necessary. Then between the age of six months and one year, the child can be weaned onto a fortified formula. Milk is a must. Specially developed soy-based infant formulae are available for the baby whose parents choose to follow a Vegan diet.

There are many soy-based milk substitutes on the market but few are suitable as the main milk for young children or pregnant and breast feeding Vegan women. Be sure to buy one which is appropriately fortified — your infant welfare nurse or a dietitian can advise you.

The Natural Alternative

There is an increased awareness of the value of good natural foods in our diet. While many parents do not wish to follow a vegetarian diet, they may want to eliminate as many artificial additives and processed foods as possible from their diet.

What are natural foods? They are fresh products grown or produced under controlled conditions to eliminate the incidence of their contact with chemicals. They are foods which come, where possible, straight from garden or farm, to your kitchen.

Organically grown fruits and vegetables come from carefully tended gardens in which only natural fertilisers are used, and to which no insecticides have been applied during their growth. No dressings are used to enhance their colours and the occasional brown spot from an insect sting may mar their appearance, but you know that these are pure products.

Grains play an important role in the natural food diet as they do in any diet. Whole grains, mixed grains and stone-ground grains are used to make breads, cakes, biscuits, cereal and pasta. The results may sometimes lack the shelf-appeal of products made with refined flours and polished grains, but their full goodness remains where their refined counterpart may have been reduced to little more than starch.

Milk products such as ricotta cheese, cottage cheese and yoghurt provide an excellent source of animal protein and are useful in making spreads, sauces and desserts.

Meats are not excluded from the natural food diet, but their consumption is usually kept to a minimum. Some butchers guarantee naturally raised meat which has not be subjected to antibiotics or artificial hormones.

Some canned and processed meats have chemicals, preservatives or colorants added and cannot be included in a natural food diet. Meat substitutes, similarly, cannot be considered truly natural food, unless manufactured from pure legumes or nuts with no additives.

Dried fruits are excellent snack foods, providing additional energy, minerals and vitamins the natural way. Check when buying certain dried fruits, particularly apricots and raisins, that liquid paraffin has not been used to prevent them sticking together.

The natural food cook will keep seasoning to a minimum.

Additionally, flour-thickened gravies may be replaced by dried bean or vegetable purées, or creamed cheeses. All canned, instant and processed foods are avoided.

A diet based on fresh fruits and vegetables, unprocessed foods and nutrient-rich unpolished grains must prove more beneficial than a highly processed one containing artificial flavours, colours and other additives and, which lacks much of the natural food value.

The natural alternative may not allow for time-saving convenience foods, but it can help your family's continuing good health.

Introducing Vegetarian Foods

Like any other child, the vegetarian baby can be offered her first solids at around four and a half to six months. These will not differ from what would be offered to a baby on an ordinary diet — rice cereal, mixed with milk or formula, unsweetened mashed banana, apple, avocado, and additional liquids in the form of fresh, fruit juices. These can be gradually increased until the eighth month, when new foods can be introduced.

Even at this stage the diet will not be noticeably different from that of a child on a regular diet. Eggs, creamed cottage cheese, a variety of fruits and vegetables, puréed dried beans and peas, milk-based desserts and cream sauces.

Meats and meat-based gravies, sauces and soups will be avoided. If the child is to be offered fish, this can take the place of meat in the diet from about seven to eight months. Meat substitutes, soy-based products and nut meats can also be included in the baby's diet. Check the labelling thoroughly, some contain high amounts of salt, MSG (monosodium glutamate) or other flavour enhancers, preservatives and artificial colourings.

Although nuts may be an important part of the adult vegetarian diet, you should not offer whole nuts to young children as they can easily choke on them.

Suitable Vegetarian Food for your Baby

A Lacto-ovo vegetarian diet for a young child can have plenty of variety, especially if parents exercise their imagination:

Eggs:
> Use often and cook in various ways, soft- or hard-boiled, poached, scrambled, omelette, steamed or baked custard. As is applicable to any other child, do not offer egg whites until the child has become accustomed to egg yolks and have shown no allergic reaction. Begin with mashed hard-boiled egg yolks, then graduate to other preparations. Never give the young child raw eggs.

Creamed cottage cheese:
> Also ricotta, soft cheese and cream cheese. Puréed or diluted with milk, these can be one of baby's staple foods.

Cereals:
> Rice, oats, millet and barley at first, then gradually introduce wheat. Home-made hot cereals and muesli.

I love little pussy, her coat is so warm,
And if I don't hurt her she'll do me no harm.
So I'll not pull her tail nor drive her away,
But pussy and I very gently will play.

Vegetarian Cassoulet and Bean Bake (opposite) with salad and bread

Pulses:

All dried beans and peas are protein-rich. Cook until tender, then purée and serve with other vegetables, dilute with milk and use in place of gravy, or make into soups.

Milk:

Offer plenty of milk puddings, milk-based sauces, soups, and milk drinks.

Fruit and Vegetables:

After the sixth month, most vegetables and fruit are acceptable.

Yoghurt:

You may want to introduce this at an earlier age than would be suitable for a child on a normal diet. After the sixth month, introduce plain unflavoured yoghurt in small quantities and watch for any reaction.

Avoid offering the small child home-made yoghurt. You may feel that it is a healthier alternative, but excess amounts of bacteria may exist in home-made yoghurt.

Remember to introduce all new foods separately and allow three or four days between each for any symptoms of intolerance to appear. If there are any signs, discontinue this food and refer to your doctor.

The foods you select for your baby will help her to grow and thrive. They will also have a marked effect on her mental growth. No undernourished baby will progress satisfactorily. Nourishment does not rely on bulk, but on the selection of foods items which will work together to build up her body, supply energy and keep her active and alert.

Careless vegetarianism can be dangerous, even fatal for a child. The damage can be done even before the baby is born. Mothers-to-be should avoid taking up a strict vegetarian diet for the first time until after the baby is born, or even until breast feeding is completed. Children born to recently converted vegetarian mothers can have inherent deficiencies. This need not be so of a practising vegetarian mother who has enjoyed the benefits of a well-balanced vegetarian diet for some time.

The following vegetarian recipes are for the whole family and are designed to serve 4–6 people.

Vegetables

Bean Bake

1 large onion, chopped
2 tablespoons butter
500 g green or French beans
1 × 375 g can three-bean mixture or red kidney beans
1 × 375 g can chickpeas (garbanzos)
1 cup (250 mL) yoghurt or sour cream
1/3 cup (75 mL) cream
1/2 cup (30 g) fresh brown breadcrumbs
butter

Sauté the onion in butter until softened. Slice the French beans and add to the onion, sauté briefly. Add the drained beans and chickpeas and mix well. Transfer to a greased casserole. Stir in the yoghurt and the cream. Cover with the lid or a piece of aluminium foil and bake in a preheated moderate oven 180°C (350°F/Gas 4) for about 25 minutes. Cover the top with the breadcrumbs and dot with butter. Return to the oven for a further 10 minutes.

Not suitable for children under 15 months.

Vegetarian Cassoulet

250 g dried haricot or kidney beans
1 large carrot
1 large onion
1 large tomato
1 stick celery
2 large potatoes
1/2 teaspoon mixed herbs

Soak the beans overnight, then drain and place in a buttered casserole. Slice the carrot, onion, tomato, celery and potatoes and add to the casserole with the herbs and sugar. Add water to cover and close the casserole or cover with a piece of aluminium foil. Bake in a moderate oven 180°C (350°F/Gas 4) for 1½ hours, adding extra water if needed.

Suitable for children from 9 months. Purée finely with some of the liquid for the younger child, and chop the vegetables for older children.

Winnie the Pooh began life as an ordinary bear taken from the shelves of Harrods department store in 1920. He was bought by Dorothy Milne for her son Christopher Robin and the bear soon became part of the family. He was named after a bear called Winnie at London zoo and a swan named Pooh. He was immortalised by Christopher's father A.A. Milne in 1926 when he wrote the classic *Winnie the Pooh*.

Sing a song of
sixpence, a pocket
full of rye,
Four and twenty
blackbirds baked in
a pie;
When the pie was
opened the birds
began to sing,
And wasn't this a
dainty dish to set
before the king?
The king was in the
counting-house
counting out his
money;
The queen was in the
parlour eating
bread and honey;
The maid was in the
garden hanging out
the clothes,
There came a little
blackbird and
nipped off her nose.

Sweet Potato Casserole

3 cups diced sweet potato or yam
½ cup (125 mL) milk
¼ cup (30 g) dry milk powder
2 eggs, beaten
¼ cup (60 mL) vegetable oil or
margarine
⅓ cup (60 g) brown sugar or honey
pinch of powdered ginger (optional)

Boil the sweet potato until tender, then
drain and blend or mash to a smooth
paste. Add the milk, milk powder, eggs
and oil and beat for a few minutes, then
add the sugar and ginger, if you are using
it. Pour into an oiled casserole and smooth
the top. Bake in a preheated moderate
oven 180°C (350°F/Gas 4) for about 45
minutes.

Suitable for children from 9 months.

Omit the ginger and use a little less
sweetening, if preferred.

Zucchini and Corn Casserole

6–8 zucchini (courgettes)
1 medium onion, chopped
2 tablespoons butter
1 × 375 g can sweet corn kernels

Cut the zucchini in halves lengthways and
scoop out the flesh with a teaspoon. Chop
and mix with the onion. Sauté the mixture
in the butter until softened, then add the
drained corn. Sauté briefly. Bring a large
saucepan of water to the boil and put
in the zucchini shells. Boil for 2 minutes,
then drain and transfer to a wide oven
dish, openings upwards. Fill with the corn
mixture. Cover with the lid or a piece
of aluminium foil and bake in a preheated
moderately hot oven 190°C (375°F/Gas
5) for about 30 minutes.

Suitable for babies over 12 months.

Asparagus with Peas

375 g fresh asparagus
1½ cups fresh or frozen peas
1 tablespoon chopped parsley
1 tablespoon butter
2 tablespoons wholemeal flour
1½ cups (375 mL) milk
2 teaspoons chopped mint

Boil the asparagus tips in lightly salted
water for 2–3 minutes, then drain. Place
in a casserole with the peas and sprinkle
on the parsley. Melt the butter in a
saucepan and add the flour. Cook for 1
minute, then add the milk and cook,
stirring, for about 4 minutes. Add the
mint. Pour the sauce over the asparagus
and peas, and place the casserole in a
moderate oven 180°C (350°F/Gas 4) to
bake until the peas are tender, about 25
minutes. Garnish with triangles of toasted
brown bread.

Mash a portion of the vegetables with
the sauce for babies from 8 months.

Broccoli with Herb Butter

500 g fresh broccoli
1 tablespoon chopped fresh herbs (parsley, chives, basil)
60 g butter

Divide the broccoli into sprigs. Steam or
boil until tender. Finely chop the herbs
and mix with the butter. Lightly sauté
in a small frying pan, until butter turns
a light golden brown color. Pour over the
broccoli, to serve.

Mash a portion of broccoli with butter
for children from 8 months, to form a
thick purée. You can also use other
cooked, mixed vegetables.

Tomato Timbales

2 cups (210 g) canned or fresh chopped
tomatoes
2 eggs, beaten
1 cup (125 g) soy flour
¼ cup (60 mL) vegetable oil or
margarine
½ cup (60 g) grated soft cheese

Mix the ingredients together, reserving a
little of the cheese, and pour into several
small oven dishes. Cover with the remaining cheese and place in a bain marie. Bake
in a preheated moderate oven 180°C
(350°F/Gas 4) for about 45 minutes.

Suitable for children from 9 months.

• Puréed canned chickpeas (garbanzos)
can be used in place of soy bean flour.

Squash and Tomato

750 g squash or zucchini (courgettes)
2 tablespoons unsalted butter
1 large onion, chopped
2 medium tomatoes, chopped

Cut the squash into cubes and fry lightly in the butter. Push to one side and fry the chopped onion until softened, then add the tomatoes. Simmer briefly, then turn into a casserole. Cook, covered for about 30 minutes in a moderate oven 180°C (350°F/Gas 4).

A topping of grated cheese and fresh breadcrumbs can be added.

Dot with butter and cook in the same way. Mash for babies under 12 months.

Cauliflower Cream

500 g fresh or frozen cauliflower
2 tablespoons butter or margarine
1 cup (250 mL) milk
2 teaspoons cornflour
2 eggs, beaten
½ cup (60 g) grated soft cheese

Finely chop the cauliflower and sauté in the butter for 2–3 minutes. Add the milk mixed with cornflour, eggs and half the cheese. Pour into several small greased oven dishes, sprinkle with the remaining cheese and place in a bain marie. Bake in a moderate oven 180°C (350°F/Gas 4) for 45 minutes.

Suitable for children from 9 months.

Sweet Potato Casserole and Asparagus with Peas (opposite)

Potatoes Baked in Cream

4 large potatoes
1 large onion
¾ cup (185 mL) cream
¼ cup (15 g) fresh brown breadcrumbs
¼ cup (30 g) grated soft cheese
butter

Peel and very thinly slice the potatoes and onion. Arrange potato layers in a greased casserole with a few rings of onion between each. Pour in the cream. Place the casserole in a moderate oven 180°C (350°F/Gas 4) to cook for about 1¼ hours. Remove and coat the top with the mixed breadcrumbs and grated cheese. Dot with butter and return to the oven to cook for a further 15 minutes.

Suitable for children from 12 months.

Spinach Custard

500 g fresh or frozen spinach
1 tablespoon butter
4 eggs
½ cup (125 mL) milk
pinch of nutmeg

Finely chop fresh spinach or thaw frozen spinach and transfer to a saucepan with the butter and 1 tablespoon water. Cover pan tightly, then simmer gently for about 7 minutes, shaking the pan from time to time. Remove and leave to cool, draining off as much water as possible. Beat the eggs and then add the milk and nutmeg. Pour over the spinach, mix well and pour into a greased casserole or into several smaller oven dishes. Set in a bain marie and bake in a moderate oven 180°C (350°F/Gas 4) for about 30 minutes, or steam for 15 minutes.

Suitable for children from 8 months.

Ideal also for finely diced celery, grated carrot, and chopped broccoli or cauliflower.

'Here we go Round the Mulberry Bush' is an acting rhyme for older toddlers. The children form a circle, take hands and dance round in a circle repeating the words of the rhyme and acting out the words by clapping hands and washing clothes.

Here we go round the
mulberry bush,
The mulberry bush,
the mulberry bush,
Here we go round the
mulberry bush,
On a cold and frosty
morning.

Salads

Fruit and Vegetable Salad with Cottage Cheese

Mix equal amounts of soaked dried fruits (prunes, sultanas, raisins, apricots and apples) with chopped celery, and fresh orange or mandarin segments. Arrange on lettuce in a salad bowl and top with a dressing made with 3 parts cottage or ricotta cheese and 1 part cream.

Grind dried fruits with cottage cheese for children under 12 months.

Bean and Rice Salad

2 cups (300 g) cooked or canned beans
(French, snake, lima, kidney, etc)
1 cup (155 g) cooked brown rice
2 teaspoons chopped parsley
2 tablespoons lemon juice or cider vinegar
2½ tablespoons vegetable oil
1¼ teaspoons honey
salt

Mix the drained beans with the rice and parsley. Shake the lemon juice or vinegar, oil, honey and salt together vigorously in a screw-top jar and pour over the salad.

Not suitable for children under 18 months.

Chickpea and Parsley Salad

1 × 440 g can chickpeas (garbanzos)
3 large tomatoes
2 tablespoons chopped parsley
2 teaspoons chopped mint
2 tablespoons lemon juice
2½ tablespoons plain yoghurt

Drain the chickpeas and place in a salad bowl. Finely chop the tomatoes and add to the peas with the chopped herbs. Mix the lemon juice and yoghurt. Stir into the salad, mixing well.

Mash the chickpeas and mix with a little yoghurt for children under 12 months. For older children, mash the peas and mix with some of the tomato and parsley and a little yoghurt.

Tabbouleh

¾ cup (155 g) cracked wheat (burghul)
3 large tomatoes
½ green capsicum (pepper)
1 small onion
2–3 tablespoons chopped parsley
2 tablespoons lemon juice
3 tablespoons vegetable or olive oil

Soak the cracked wheat overnight, then drain and transfer to a salad bowl. Finely chop the tomatoes, capsicum and onion and mix with the wheat and parsley. Shake the lemon juice and oil together in a screw-top jar and pour over the salad.

Suitable for children over 18 months.

Cucumber and Yoghurt Salad

1 large cucumber
1 spring onion, optional
1 tablespoon chopped parsley
1 teaspoon chopped fresh mint
1 cup (250 mL) plain yoghurt
1 teaspoon sugar

Peel the cucumber and grate finely, discarding the seed core. Very finely chop the spring onion and mix with the cucumber and remaining ingredients. Beat for 1 minute, then chill thoroughly. For children under 12 months, omit the herbs.

A refreshing side dish to serve with grilled fish and stewed vegetables.

Apple and Mandarin Salad

1 × 315 g can mandarin segments
1–2 red apples
½ cup (90 g) raisins
1/3 cup honey

Drain the mandarins and place in a salad bowl. Peel, core and slice or chop the apples and add to the salad. Scatter on the raisins and mix in lightly. Mix the yoghurt and honey and pour over salad.

Suitable for children over 12 months.

Fruit and Vegetable Salad with Cottage Cheese (opposite)

Spreads

The following recipes are for delicious vegetable and cheese spreads which can be served with toast, crackers or crispbread and as dips.

Bean and Cheese Spread

Heat 375 g of red kidney beans in the liquid from the can until boiling. Drain and mash. Sauté a finely chopped medium onion in 1 tablespoon of butter until soft and lightly coloured. Mash and add the beans. Stir in 1 cup (125 g) of grated Cheddar or other cheese. If liked, 1–2 finely chopped tomatoes can be added, sautéing in the butter until tender. Great with corn chips.

Tomato, Onion and Cheese Spread

Sauté 1 cup (145 g) of finely chopped onion in 2 tablespoons butter until soft and lightly coloured. Add 1¼–1½ cups (260 g) finely chopped skinned tomatoes and cook until tender. Add 1–2 teaspoons of fresh, chopped herbs. Remove from the heat and beat in 2 egg yolks mixed with 1 tablespoon cream and ¾–1 cup (90–125 g) of grated cheese. Return to low heat and beat until the cheese is melted. Store for 3–4 days in the refrigerator.

Cheese Spread

Bring ⅔ cup (155 mL) milk to the boil in the top of a double saucepan. Add a beaten large egg and 2½–3 cups (315–375 g) of grated Cheddar or other cheese. Season with a pinch of mustard powder and stir until well mixed and the cheese is melted, then beat for about 15 minutes. Store for up to 1 week in the refrigerator.

Cottage Cheese Spread

Mash cottage cheese or ricotta with grated onion, snipped chives, crushed garlic, chopped parsley, smooth peanut butter, honey, mashed banana or chopped tomato, according to your taste. Store in the refrigerator for up to 1 week.

When giving parties, try to be well organised without being too rigid about things. Some games, such as pass the parcel, may be so popular that the children want them three times. Others may not appeal at all. Stay flexible — little kids love just being at a party. A few balloons, a cake, and something to take home is all they really need to have a wonderfully exciting time.

Eggs

Eggs en Cocotte with Tomato and Cheese

Prepare a recipe of *Tomato, Onion and Cheese Spread* (on this page) and pour half into a greased shallow oven dish. Make 4–6 depressions in the spread and break a fresh egg into each. Cover with the remaining spread and top with a sprinkling of fresh breadcrumbs. Bake in a preheated moderate oven 180°C (350°F/Gas 4) for about 20 minutes.

Suitable for children over 18 months.

Devilled Eggs

4 large eggs
1 tablespoon cottage or ricotta cheese
1½ teaspoons tomato purée
pinch of chopped fresh basil or parsley

Hard-boil the eggs, then cool and cut in halves lengthways. Remove the yolks and mash with the cheese, tomato purée and herbs. Spoon the mixture back into the egg white cases and chill.

Suitable for children from 12 months. Omit the herbs if preferred.

Add a large pinch of chilli powder or cayenne pepper to give a good hot taste to the filling, for older children.

Tuna-stuffed Eggs

6 eggs
90 g canned tuna
1 tablespoon mayonnaise
1 teaspoon finely chopped red capsicum

Hard-boil the eggs and cut in halves lengthways. Drain and flake the tuna and mix with the egg yolks, mayonnaise and chopped capsicum, working until thoroughly mixed. Spoon back into the egg white cases and serve on shredded lettuce.

Suitable for children from 12 months. If preferred, omit the capsicum.

Home-made Baked Beans (page 93) and Eggs en Cocotte with Tomato and Cheese (opposite)   91

Scrambled Eggs with Sweet Corn Sauce

1 × 250 g can sweet corn kernels
1 tablespoon butter
1 cup (250 mL) milk
2 teaspoons cornflour
6 eggs
1 tablespoon milk

Lightly crush the corn in a food processor or blender. Melt the butter in a saucepan and add the corn. Sauté briefly, then add the milk mixed with the cornflour and bring to the boil. Simmer, stirring until the sauce thickens.

Beat the eggs and milk together and add a large pinch of salt and a little pepper. Melt 1–2 teaspoons butter in a frying pan and pour in the egg. Cook gently, stirring occasionally, until just firm. Transfer to a plate and pour on the sauce.

Suitable for children from 18 months. The corn can be puréed finely and passed through a sieve to serve to younger children.

Grilled Fish with Sweet Corn Sauce (above)

Fish

Grilled Fish with Sweet Corn Sauce

Season fish fillets with a little lemon juice. Brush with melted butter and grill on both sides until cooked. Prepare the *Sweet Corn Sauce* from the previous recipe and pour over the fish before serving.

Suitable for children from 18 months. The fish can be puréed and the sauce passed through a sieve to serve to younger children.

Fish Baked with Yoghurt

6 whiting fillets (approx. 410 g)
1 cup (60 g) fresh wholemeal breadcrumbs
lemon juice
¾ cup (185 mL) plain yoghurt
¼ cup (60 mL) water
2 teaspoons cornflour
½ teaspoon caraway seeds (optional)

Grease a casserole and coat lightly with breadcrumbs, reserving some. Season the fillets with lemon juice and place half in the casserole. Top with another layer of crumbs, then add the remaining fish and finish with crumbs. Mix the yoghurt, water, cornflour and caraway seeds together and pour down the sides of the dish. Set in a moderate oven 180°C (350°F/Gas 4) and bake for about 30 minutes.

Sour cream can be used instead of yoghurt.

Suitable for children from 9 months; can be puréed or chopped as required.

Tuna Mousse

2 teaspoons unflavoured gelatine
¼ cup (60 mL) cool water
¾ cup (185 mL) boiling water
1 small onion, finely chopped
1 teaspoon lemon juice
¼ teaspoon dill tips
1–2 tablespoons finely chopped red capsicum
1 × 220 g can tuna
1/3 cup (75 mL) mayonnaise

Sprinkle the gelatine over the cool water and leave for 5–6 minutes to soften, then add the boiling water and stir until the gelatine has dissolved.

Place the remaining ingredients in a blender and blend at high speed to a smooth purée, then add the gelatine liquid. Add a little extra water if the mixture is very thick.

Wet a 2 cup jelly mould and pour in the tuna mixture. Refrigerate until set.

Suitable for children from 15 months.

Rice, Dried Beans and Pasta

Home-made Baked Beans

3 cups (540 g) soya beans
3 cups (315 g) chopped canned or fresh tomatoes
1 cup (250 mL) vegetable stock
1 bay leaf
2 tablespoons chopped parsley
pinch of dried thyme
vegetable oil

Cook the soya beans in plenty of water until tender, about 4 hours. Drain. Transfer to a greased casserole and add the tomato, stock and the seasonings. Add about 2 tablespoons vegetable oil and cover the casserole. Bake in a preheated moderate oven 180°C (350°F/Gas 4) for about 40 minutes.

Suitable for children over 15 months. Mash before serving, if necessary.

Dhal

1½ cups (300 g) yellow or red lentils (or split peas)
4 cups (1 litre) cold water
1 bay leaf
1 medium onion
2 tablespoons butter
2 tablespoons thick cream
1-2 teaspoons chopped parsley
2 hard-boiled egg yolks (optional)

Wash the lentils or peas and place in a saucepan with the water and bay leaf. Boil until tender, then drain and mash. Finely chop the onion and sauté in the butter until softened, then add the mashed lentils and the cream and parsley or sieved egg yolks, if used. Discard the bay leaf. Beat until smooth and creamy.

Suitable for children from 8 months, using the egg yolk instead of parsley.

Mary had a little lamb
With fleece as white as snow.
And everywhere that Mary went
The lamb was sure to go.

Baked Brown Rice with Tomato and Cheese

1½ cups (250 g) brown rice
1 large onion
2 tablespoons butter or vegetable oil
1½ cups (260 g) chopped tomatoes
2 teaspoons chopped parsley
2 cups (500 mL) milk or vegetable stock
1 cup (125 g) grated soft cheese

Cook the rice in plenty of water until tender. Drain. Sauté the finely chopped onion in the butter until soft, then add the tomatoes and parsley and cook until tender. Add the rice and transfer to a greased casserole and pour on the milk. Add half the grated cheese, stirring in lightly. Cover and bake in a moderate oven 180°C (350°F/Gas 4) for about 25 minutes, then remove the lid, add the remaining cheese to cover the top and bake again until the top is golden.

Remove baby's portion before adding the cheese topping and mash or purée to serve. Suitable for children from 10 months.

Tuna and Tomato Risotto

1 large onion
2 tablespoons vegetable oil or butter
2 sticks celery
1½ cups (250 g) long grain rice
2 teaspoons chopped fresh herbs
1 × 375 g can tuna
1 × 375 g can tomatoes, chopped
2 cups (500 mL) tomato juice or vegetable stock
1–2 teaspoons chopped parsley

Finely chop the onion and sauté in the oil until soft. Add finely chopped celery and sauté briefly, then add the rice and sauté until transparent. Add the herbs and the tomato juice and simmer, covered, over low heat until the liquid is below the level of the rice. Add the flaked tuna and chopped tomatoes and the liquid from the tomatoes. Cover and cook until the rice is tender and fluffy, then stir the tuna and tomato lightly into the rice, adding the chopped parsley.

Suitable for children over 12 months. Mash or purée before serving.

Sliced fresh mushrooms can be added with the tomato.

Wholemeal Macaroni Cheese

185 g wholemeal macaroni
1½ tablespoons butter
2½ tablespoons wholemeal flour
2 cups (500 mL) milk
1½ tablespoons dry milk powder
1¼ cups (155 g) grated soft cheese
1 large onion

Boil the macaroni in water until tender, drain and transfer to a greased casserole. Melt the butter in a saucepan and add the flour. Cook for 1 minute, then add the milk mixed with the milk powder and boil, stirring for 4–5 minutes. Add the cheese and cook until melted. Finely chop the onion, sauté in a little butter or vegetable oil until soft and lightly coloured. Pour over the macaroni, then cover with the sauce. Bake in a preheated moderate oven 180°C (350°F/Gas 4) for about 20 minutes. A topping of fresh breadcrumbs mixed with grated cheese can be added and cooked until crisp and golden.

Suitable for children from 12 months.

Rice and Bean Loaf

1½ cups (250 g) brown rice
2 tablespoons butter or vegetable oil
1 medium onion, finely chopped
1 clove garlic, crushed
2 large tomatoes, chopped
½ cup (90 g) red kidney beans or cannellini (butter beans)
2 cups diced mixed vegetables (carrots, beans, peas, parsnips, squash)
3 cups (750 mL) vegetable stock
1 bay leaf

Sauté the rice in the butter or oil for 1–2 minutes. Transfer to a greased casserole. Add the onion and garlic to the pan and sauté briefly, then add the tomatoes and beans and sauté for 1–2 minutes. Transfer to the casserole and add the diced vegetables, stock and seasonings. Cover the casserole, cook in a preheated moderate oven 180°C (350°F/Gas 4) until the rice is tender and liquid has been absorbed, about 45 minutes. A topping of fresh breadcrumbs with grated cheese can be added, bake until crisp and golden.

Suitable for children over 12 months. Remove the child's portion before the topping is added, and purée if needed.

Little Miss Muffet
Sat on a tuffet,
Eating some curds
and whey;
There came a great
spider,
And sat down beside
her,
And frightened Miss
Muffet away.

Rice and Bean Loaf (opposite), Tuna and Tomato Risotto (opposite) and Lentil Soup (page 96)

Soup

Split Pea or Lentil Soup

1¼ cups (250 g) dried lentils or split peas
5 cups (1.25 L) vegetable stock or beef tea
1 medium onion
2-3 medium tomatoes
¾ teaspoon dried mixed herbs

Soak the lentils or peas overnight, then drain and place in a saucepan with the stock, finely chopped onion and tomatoes, and herbs. Bring to the boil and simmer until the peas are tender.

● To make a rich spicy lentil soup, add curry powder and thickened cream; and 1 teaspoon chopped fresh mint and a little sugar for a tasty pea soup.

Suitable for children from 8 months. Omit the herbs, if preferred.

Red Bean and Rice Soup

315 g dried red kidney beans
5½ cups (1.4 L) water or vegetable stock
1 bay leaf
½ cup (90 g) long grain rice
250 g French beans
2 tablespoons vegetable oil
1 clove garlic, crushed
1 large onion, finely chopped
1 cup chopped canned or fresh tomatoes
1 teaspoon brown sugar
2 teaspoons lemon juice
chopped parsley

Soak the beans overnight, then drain and transfer to a large saucepan. Add the water and bay leaf, boil for 2 minutes and simmer until tender, about 1¾ hours. Add the rice and beans cut into short pieces and simmer for about 18 minutes, adding additional water or vegetable stock if needed. Heat the oil and dry the garlic and onion until softened, then add the tomatoes, sugar and lemon juice. Pour into the soup and simmer for 5–6 minutes. Add parsley before serving.

Suitable for children from 8 months. Purée some of the beans and rice with soup stock to serve.

Sweet Dishes and Pastries

Sultana Turnovers

125 g butter
½ cup (90 g) icing sugar
a few drops imitation vanilla essence
1 cup (125 g) wholemeal self-raising flour
½ cup (60 g) cornflour
2 teaspoons milk
Filling:
2 tablespoons sultanas (seedless raisins)

Cream the butter and icing sugar together, then add the vanilla essence. Sift in the flours and add the milk. Mix well and knead lightly. Cover with plastic wrap and refrigerate for 1 hour, then roll out very thinly and cut into 6 cm rounds using a fluted cutter. Place a spoonful of sultanas in the centre of each biscuit. Run a wet finger around the edge of the biscuits, then fold over to encase the filling and pinch the edges together. Arrange on a lightly greased biscuit tray and bake in a preheated moderate oven 180°C (350°F/Gas 4) for 12 minutes. Remove from the tray, dust with icing sugar while still warm and leave to cool on a rack. Store in an airtight container.

Apple Wheat Crumble

500 g stewed apples
1 tablespoon honey
1 tablespoon raw wheatgerm
3 tablespoons crushed wholemeal biscuits
2 tablespoons raw sugar
2 tablespoons butter

Pour the apple into a greased pie dish and drizzle on the honey. Mix the wheatgerm, biscuit crumbs and sugar together and spread thickly over the fruit. Dot with the butter and bake in a preheated moderate oven 180°C (350°F/Gas 4) for about 20 minutes until heated through and the top is browned.

● Stewed dried apricots can be used in place of, or with the apple.

Wholemeal Fruit Puffs

½ cup (125 mL) vegetable oil
1 cup (500 mL) boiling water
1 cup (125 g) wholemeal plain flour
4 eggs
1 cup puréed fruit
125 g cream cheese

Pour the oil and boiling water into the top of a double saucepan and add the flour. Beat vigorously over hot water until the mixture is smooth and thick and does not stick to the pan. Remove from the heat and leave to cool for 20 minutes, then beat the eggs into the mixture, separately, working until thoroughly mixed.

Rub a baking sheet with an oiled cloth. Spoon tablespoons of the mixture onto the sheet, allowing space between each for expansion. Bake in a preheated hot oven 230°C (450°F/Gas 8) for about 30 minutes until puffed and cooked right through. They should be dry on the inside.

Remove from the tray and leave to cool. Fill with a mixture of puréed fresh or canned fruit mixed with the cream cheese.

Apricot Fool

250 g dried apricots
1½ cups (375 mL) plain yoghurt
⅔ cup (155 mL) thickened cream
½ orange
brown sugar or honey (optional)

Soak the apricots overnight in water to cover, then simmer in the same water until tender. Blend, using just enough water to make a thick purée. Add the yoghurt and cream and the finely grated rind of the half orange. Sweeten to taste with brown sugar or honey. Chill. To serve, garnish with the fine shreds of orange peel which have been blanched in boiling water and thoroughly drained.

Apple Wheat Crumble with custard, and Wholemeal Fruit Puffs (above)

Food for Special Occasions

Travelling with baby, eating at restaurants, lunchbox meals, children's parties and quick healthy snacks for big appetites are covered in this chapter of hints, recipes, menus and surprises.

SPECIAL OCCASIONS ARE TIMES for house rules about nutrition to be suspended, though not completely forgotten.

A child's first Christmas or birthday is of no consequence to him, and food will be made for older children and adult guests. Possibly all that will interest a one-year-old will be the candles on the cake, which he will probably try to eat.

Party Time

By the second birthday, however, party time does mean something — cakes, cookies and candies. Your child's capacity for stowing away large amounts of these may surprise you.

Avoid making the mistake of having only sweet food on the party table, as children do enjoy savoury snacks. Always set the table with savoury foods to be offered *before* bringing out the sweet foods. Crisps, pretzels and cheesy straws are popular, as well as meatballs, cold meats and a variety of sandwiches and dips.

Birthday cakes should look great but not be too rich or oversweet. Butter cream icing is ideal for creating imaginative cake shapes and decorations but it often goes uneaten, even by the most dedicated sweet tooth. Try instead a mild gingerbread man or gingerbread house, a chocolate cake or a sponge gaily decorated with a thin icing and or coloured sprinkles. If you do want to be sensible but still give your child a treat, whip up a carrot cake and top it with cream cheese dressing.

Cakes

Fun birthday cakes for the one- or two-year-old could include a large number one or two; ice-cream shaped into a boat, duck, chicken, beach ball; a simple sponge cake topped with whipped cream and sandwiched with jam; a plain chocolate cake with colourful icing; or a gingerbread man or teddy bear made with chocolate crackle mixture.

Decorations should be colourful and edible like chopped jelly beans, chocolate or carob bits, coloured sprinkles, coconut coloured with food dyes, marshmallow flowers.

To make marshmallow flowers, cut marshmallows into slices, about three

Jack and Jill went up the hill
To fetch a pail of water;
Jack fell down and broke his crown,
And Jill came tumbling after.

slices per marshmallow, and dip the cut sides into coloured sprinkles or jelly crystals. Stick the petal together to make four for five-petalled flowers and place a coloured sweet in the centre.

Use clear honey as the 'glue' for cake decorations as an alternative to icing.

Extras

Other party foods can include simple sandwiches with fillings young children enjoy — smooth peanut butter, Vegemite (Marmite), chopped egg, ham or chicken. Also serve open sandwiches decorated with coloured sprinkles. Avoid popcorn, hard sweets and corn chips. These can all cause problems of choking.

For drinks, offer home-made party punch; blackcurrant syrup mixed with lemonade or soda water; apple or grape juice diluted with soda water or plain mineral water; concentrated orange juice whipped with milk.

Serve drinks in plastic or paper cups with straws. Include pieces of fresh fruit in the punch and give out spoons, or small forks for spearing them.

Activities

Organised games are not appreciated by children of these ages, so instead set out plenty of toys, bikes or pedal cars so they can organise their own activities.

If the other mothers agree, and the weather is warm, finger painting with large blobs of paint in low tables set out in the garden, or water games involving bubble blowing are fun. Bring bathing costumes and towels.

Later Birthdays

The third and fourth birthdays are important events and your child will enjoy participating in the preparations for his special day. Choose at least one food which he can help to make and allow him to assist with the decoration of the room, table and food.

Aim for a balance of sweet and savoury dishes on the table. The cake will be the feature, and should be one which the children will enjoy eating afterwards.

Novelty items are appreciated, and

many can be made well in advance. Consider the following:

- Crackers (bonbons) made from discarded kitchen roll centres and crêpe paper. Fill with sweets, crisps, a balloon or perhaps some small toys.
- Party pies made into sailing boats using coloured card and wooden sticks.
- Fancy sandwiches — pinwheels, layers, cut-outs, fairy bread.
- Animal shapes in meringue or pastry.
- Faces on ice-creams using icing or chocolate.
- Scooped out orange skins filled with fruit jelly or frozen yoghurt.
- Snails made from sliced chocolate Swiss roll.
- A cookie tree (also great for Christmas).
- Mice made from cream-cheese-filled prunes.
- Cubes of cold meat threaded on to pretzels.

Organised games may now be enjoyed. If you don't know any, ask the kindergarten or pre-school teacher for suggestions. Children will also enjoy showing off some of their newly acquired skills learned at their kindergarten.

Pinwheel Sandwiches (page 102)

Party Menus

1 Mini Drumsticks
  Pitta Roll-ups
  Fairy Bread

  Prune Mice
  Muesli Crunch Biscuits

  Ice-cream Cake (bought)
  Apple and Grape Juice mixed with soda water

2 Layered Sandwiches
  Dish of crisps
  Dish of pretzels
  Variety of dips

  Cup Cakes with coloured sprinkles

  Carrot Cake
  Apricot Orange Whizz

3 Cold Meat roll-ups
  Pinwheel Sandwiches
  Dish of crisps
  Variety of dips

  Apple Cup Cakes
  Oatmeal Biscuits

  Chocolate Cake (your favourite recipe)
  Blackcurrant Fizz

4 Meatballs
  Cut-out Sandwiches
  Dish of cheese crisps
  Variety of dips

  Orange Jelly Baskets
  Ice-cream

  Sponge Cake
  Honey Shakes

(See Index for the recipes).

Party Sandwiches

Use smooth spreads such as fish paste, cream cheese with chopped parsley, mashed boiled egg, crab paste, smooth peanut butter, Vegemite (Marmite), cheese spread. Use white, wholemeal and brown bread to give interesting variety.

Pinwheel Sandwiches

Remove the crusts from a very fresh loaf of white or brown (wholemeal) bread. Cut thin slices lengthways. Spread each slice with a contrasting spread, such as cream (Marmite) or crab paste on white bread.

Roll each slice up separately to give long thin rolls and wrap in plastic wrap to keep from unrolling. Refrigerate for at least 1 hour to set into the roll. To serve, cut each roll into bite-sized pieces.

Layered Sandwiches

Make sandwiches using 2 slices of white, 2 slices of brown and 1–2 slices of multi-grain bread. Spread with different coloured spreads, stack together with the different breads layered alternately. Remove the crusts. Cut through each stack from top to bottom, cutting into squares which will give square fingers of different layered breads.

Cut-out Sandwiches

Use biscuit cutters to stamp out different shapes in made-up sandwiches. Use both brown and white breads and a variety of fillings. If you have two different sizes of any one shape, such as hearts, triangles, or circles, make up an even number of brown and white sandwiches, and stamp the larger size from each of the sandwiches. Then from the centre of each shape stamp out the same smaller shape and remove the inner piece. Switch these around so that a brown sandwich now has a white centre and vice versa.

Cold Meat Roll-ups

Use thin slices of ham, roast beef, pork or luncheon meat. Roll each slice around a tasty filling such as grated carrot mixed with cream cheese or mayonnaise, relish, mashed potato, mashed boiled egg, sticks of fresh or canned vegetable. Secure with toothpicks or roll each up with plastic wrap and refrigerate until set in place.

Meatballs

Mix together 500 g of very finely minced lean beef, 2 tablespoons plain (all-purpose) flour, 1 egg yolk, 2 tablespoons cream and 1 tablespoon grated onion. Add 1–2 tablespoons fresh breadcrumbs and work the mixture until smooth. Shape into small balls and shallow fry in a mixture of butter and vegetable oil, or dip into egg then coat with dry breadcrumbs and deep fry until golden. Serve hot or cold. Makes approximately 30.

Little Boy Blue, come blow your horn, The sheep's in the meadow, the cow's in the corn. What! Is this the way you mind your sheep, Under the haycock fast asleep?

Prune Mice

Slit open prunes, remove the stones and fill the cavities with cream cheese sweetened with a little honey. Cut long thin strips of licorice for the tails and add two points of pink musk stick sweet at the other end to resemble ears. Thin licorice can be cut for whiskers.

Ice-Cream Faces

Make large round scoops of ice-cream and place on a biscuit tray which will fit into your freezer. Use coloured icing or buttercream, or dark cooking chocolate to pipe facial features on one side of each ball of ice-cream — eyes, nose, mouth. Add straight hair, curls or a hat. Keep in the freezer until ready to serve, then place in ice-cream cones or shallow dishes.

Orange Jelly Baskets

Select good oranges and cut a wedge from two sides of each, leaving a loop across the centre-top to form a handle. Carefully scrape out the flesh leaving just the shell with the handle. Prepare an orange or lemon flavoured jelly using slightly less liquid than the instructions on the package advise. Pour into the orange baskets, then leave to cool. Refrigerate until set and do not remove from the refrigerator until ready to serve.

As an alternative, fill the orange cases with frozen fruit yoghurt.

Jelly Baskets and Ice-Cream Faces (above)

Teddy Bears are loved the world over by people of all ages. One of the best loved bears must be Paddington Bear, found on Paddington rail station, London, in 1956 after arriving from Peru with only a duffel coat, hat, wellington boots and a note to say 'Please look after this bear. Thank you'. Michael Bond was Paddington's creator. After seeing a single, lonely bear on a shelf in a large department store, he bought the bear for his wife and then he wrote the story of Paddington Bear. Today Paddington can be seen on over two hundred products ranging from children's clothing, wallpaper and furnishing fabrics to china and chocolates.

Travelling with Baby

The nursing mother has a distinct advantage over her bottle-feeding counterpart when away from home, either for a day's outing or a holiday. With some simple preparations, however, travelling with your baby should be trouble free.

Air Travel

Most airlines, particularly international companies, cater well to the mother's and baby's needs. The cabin staff will assist with the heating and washing of bottles, and mixing of formula, and offer additional services to ensure your comfort.

Check ahead with the airline and request a bulk-head seat. These are situated just behind the galley or toilet block and allow plenty of leg room. If your baby is small, a bassinet will be provided on request. This clips safely on to the wall in front of you, giving easy access to the baby. A mesh safety net can be fastened over the bassinet for security. Blankets and extra pillows can be made available to you and often there's a free mother's comfort kit.

I once received a quite comprehensive kit from an Asian airline, which included a half dozen disposable nappies (diapers), each with a plastic bag and a twist tie for storage after use, a face cloth, cotton buds and cottonwool balls, and small bottles of baby lotion, baby oil and talcum powder. All of this packed into a stylish zip-top carry bag which has since become my daughter's personal toilet bag for use whenever we travel.

Extra hand baggage is usually allowed for the mother with a child. Up to the age of two, or even three on some airlines, children travel free of charge and are expected to sit on their mother's knee. While the baby is small, you may enjoy greater comfort by using a chest sling, which removes the weight from your legs. Recline the seat so that your baby is lying on your chest, you should be able to enjoy the flight in comfort.

Food and drink for the baby on board might include plain milk, boiled water and unsweetened fruit juices, usually available at no cost. Additionally, if the baby is eating solids you may choose to

share your own meal, if suitable.

Most airline meals are lightly seasoned and usually consist of good wholesome meats, light gravies and boiled vegetables. As well there may be fruit or a fruit dessert and cheese, and there is usually a fresh breadroll, butter and crackers.

Snack meals on short trips are usually sweet biscuits, buns or cakes which are not usually suitable for the baby. This is a time when jars of commercial baby food are a boon.

During the Flight

Remember to offer the child sufficient liquids. Aeroplane travel usually results in mild dehydration, so give plenty of water and perhaps increase the usual feedings of milk or formula. Additional orange or apple juice as well can counter the possibility of milk constipation, which is not an uncommon after effect of flying.

More than anything, relax and enjoy the trip. The staff are there to help you, even though your child may be a non-paying passenger. Don't worry too much about disturbing your fellow passengers. You'll find that most will be sympathetic and understanding, even if the baby does begin to yell in the middle of the night.

Your child may experience ear discomfort during ascent and descent. Babies should be offered breast or bottle during this time as the sucking motion will help to break the pressure build-up. As well, you will feel more comfortable with the baby safely and securely in your arms.

Give older children a sweet to suck, or hold their noses closed and ask them to blow gently through their noses to relieve the pressure. If your child is old enough, chewing gum is good in these situations.

Travelling by Car, Bus or Train

If you're planning a lengthy trip overland, equip yourself with a small cooler — the polyurethane 6-pack beer cooler is ideal, especially if it has a freezable sealed plastic cooling block. These can be frozen each night in your motel bedroom fridge, or ask the hotel management to freeze them for you overnight. They will keep the contents of the cooler quite cold through-

Travelling with baby

Consult your maternal and child health professional for more detailed advice on travelling with your baby or toddler.

out the day. In this you can store water to make up the day's formula, also bottles, teats, fruit juice and food.

If bottle sterilisation is still on your agenda, take along a rigid plastic storage container and a small container of sterilising solution. Sterilise the utensils in the container each evening. After sterilisation and disposal of the solution, store utensils in the container for travelling.

For even greater convenience, purchase a pack of disposable bottle liners and take just one bottle and several teats. The bottle will need rinsing in hot water after each use. Teats can be sterilised in a small plastic container with a well fitted lid. Leave the sterilised teats in the container, without the sterilising solution, for travel.

Use the electric jug or kettle provided in your hotel or motel room to boil water for the following day's formula. Transfer it to a sterilised 1 litre plastic soft drink bottle or a thermos flask, depending on whether you require the water at room temperature or warmer; or simply measure into the bottles you will be using. It's convenient then to add the formula when baby is ready for a bottle.

It is safe practice not to make up formula in the morning, even if you do have a reasonably efficient cooler. The milk could begin to spoil, and a stomach upset could result.

Can I Trust the Water when Travelling?

If there are any doubts about the quality of the water in the places you'll be staying or passing through, buy up ready-made formula in cans for the duration of the trip. A prepared soy bean milk formula is also available in a carton with straw. Introduce it to your baby several days before you leave home, to ensure that the transition will be trouble free.

Thoroughly boiled water should be reasonably bacteria free but if in doubt, use bottled water.

Water purifying tablets can be used but they may impart a slight taste. This is acceptable to most babies.

Food for the Trip

The young infant will be happy with a repetitive and convenient diet of cereal, bottled fruit or vegetables, the occasional banana and juice as a supplement to bottle or breast milk.

The toddler, however, may be more demanding. Keep a supply of easy snack foods on hand, and be flexible about ideal diets for the duration of the trip. No child is going to suffer a major setback in health by having a fast-food diet for a few days.

Easy snacks are cracker biscuits and crispbreads; individually wrapped cheese sticks; tiny packs of sultanas (seedless raisins); snack sized pop-top canned fruits; small tubs of yoghurt or cottage cheese; individually wrapped small packs of sweet biscuits; small squeeze-packs of fruit juices with straws; bottled and canned baby foods; bananas, apples, grapes.

Pack several feeder bibs, bowl and spoon and training cup. A sheet of plastic or an old towel can be placed under the chair during meals in your hotel bedroom to prevent spoiling the carpet, or feed the baby in the kitchen.

Your child's car seat can double as a baby chair if it has a metal support at the back to hold it upright.

Take along several small plastic containers with vacuum-sealed lids. Store portions of your leftover lunch to give to the baby for dinner. Keep only foods which are plainly cooked without sauces, and avoid meat unless it is of the simple, roasted kind. Store it well chilled in your cooler, next to the frozen cooler block, for not more than about five hours.

Don't take chances with your baby's health. Unless you're able to refrigerate the food immediately, and serve it straight from the refrigerator, do not attempt to keep the remains of any meals. It is better to make up a fresh lot.

Remember the invaluable egg. Your child may be happy to eat eggs often. Ask the hotel or motel management to boil a couple of eggs to take with you the next day.

Eating at a Restaurant or Fast-food Outlet

If you take your child with you to a restaurant, request a high chair and ask for the meal to be served quickly. Children do not usually enjoy sitting around, particularly if they are hungry.

Look over the menu for foods which would be suitable. Vegetables are usually thoroughly cooked at restaurants. These can be chopped or mashed with a little milk or formula. Look also through the sweets offered. Custards, rice puddings and other mild-flavoured puddings can be acceptable.

Breakfast menus usually offer plenty for the child — cereals, eggs, toast, sausages.

Alternatively, simply bring along your own can or jar of baby food and a spoon. The restaurant is unlikely to object.

The majority of fast-food restaurants have at least some dishes suitable for the young child. I have always found fish a good standby. Fried fish, when its crumb coating or batter is removed, is moist, tender and not oily. Mashed potato and gravy come with many chicken take-aways, and many children enjoy chips (French fries).

A hamburger, minus the bun and trimmings, is tasty and can be chopped to a reasonably fine consistency.

The baby's basic diet may be makeshift, but by offering plenty of fresh fruit, milk and cheese you can achieve a reasonable balance.

Hints to make Holidaying Easier

- Pack and use disposable nappies (diapers) or a nappy washing service throughout your holiday.
- Use disposable premoistened cloths for small clean-up jobs.
- Travel as light as possible. Comfort is more important than fashion.
- Don't forget your child's special friend, such as baby blanket, soft toy, etc, or you could have difficulties at night.
- Pack hats, sunscreen, insect repellent, a warm jumper even if it's the middle of summer, and an umbrella.
- Always offer your child plenty of liquids, especially when on the beach, or travelling on hot days.
- Take a pack of plastic bags with twist ties. They are useful for storing food scraps, used disposable nappies, your own bits and pieces and for carrying filled bottles — better to leak in the bag than to soak the contents of your handbag.

Eating out: breakfast

ADDITIVE: any substance added to a product, usually to preserve or alter its quality.

ALLERGIC REACTION: hypersensitivity to certain substances e.g. cats, pollen, grasses, some foods; if severe, requires medical attention.

ALLSPICE: a mildly sharp, fragrant spice, not to be confused with mixed spice.

ALPHABET NOODLES: pasta noodles made in the shape of alphabet letters.

ANTIPASTO: hors d'oeuvre or appetiser, Italian in origin, usually of smoked fish, cold meats, pickles and olives.

ARROWROOT: a fine, starchy flour, used as a thickening agent. Cornflour (cornstarch) can be used as a substitute.

BABY CLINIC: special clinics set up to provide professional medical advice and support for parents and babies; most local government authorities have one — check with your local council or hospital.

BAIN MARIE: An oven dish containing warm water which comes halfway up the sides of cups or baking dishes in which food is being cooked.

BICARBONATE OF SODA: baking soda, an ingredient of baking powder.

BISCUITS: cookies.

BOUQUET GARNI: mixture of herbs, usually including parsley, thyme and bay leaf, and sometimes also including a stalk of celery, a piece of carrot and a few peppercorns. Some cooks make their own muslin bags, to dangle in casseroles and remove after cooking, some buy them ready-made, some people simply add the herbs directly to whatever they are cooking and remove only the bay leaf when ready to serve. Bay leaves should be removed as they remain rigid and can cause choking.

BRAN CEREAL: a breakfast cereal made from bran — the ground husks of grain.

BUTTERMILK: slightly sour liquid left from separating cream. Skim milk can be substituted.

CAPSICUM: red or green pepper.

CARDAMOM: an aromatic, Asian spice. Anise or cinnamon can be substituted.

CASSEROLE: a stew, cooked by slow simmering over low heat for a few hours.

CAYENNE PEPPER: a very hot spice ground from several kinds of capsicum (pepper).

CHEESE: Ricotta: use cheese with 10% fat content.
Tasty: use matured cheese.
Parmesan: best grated fresh; can use any strong-flavoured cheese.

CINNAMON: a mildly pungent spice, used as a ground powder, or as sticks ('quills').

CLOVES: a sharp, aromatic spice, used whole or ground.

COCONUT, DESSICATED: finely shredded dried coconut.

COLOSTRUM: rich milk-like fluid produced by nursing mothers in the first few days after birth; contains special antibodies to protect the baby.

COPHA: a form of purified coconut oil, also sold as coconut butter, Copha Butter and Kremelta (registered trademarks).

CORNFLOUR: cornstarch.

CRACKERS: dry biscuits.

CREAM: also known as single, light or coffee cream.
Thickened cream: double, heavy or whipping cream.

Sour cream: soured or dairy sour cream, also available in fat-reduced form.
Scalded cream: cream brought briefly to boiling point.

CREAM OF TARTAR: potassium bitartrate, an ingredient of baking powder.

EGGPLANT: aubergine.

ESSENCE: extract.

EVAPORATED MILK: thick, unsweetened milk made by reducing the water content.

FINGER FOODS: any food a baby or young toddler can eat while holding in the hand, such as rusks.

FLOUR: use plain (all-purpose) flour unless otherwise specified.
Self-raising flour: all-purpose flour with baking powder added in the proportion of 1 cup (250 g) flour to 1 teaspoon (5 g) baking powder.
Wholemeal flour: wholewheat all-purpose or self-raising flour.

FOLD: to combine a mixture with other ingredients while retaining lightness, by gently turning one part over another with a spoon or spatular.

FORMULA: commercially prepared milk for young babies, usually made up with water following directions from a baby health professional.

GINGER, GROUND: powdered ginger, a strongly pungent spice.

GLACÉ FRUITS: fruits coated with sugar to give an attractive edible finish.

GOLDEN SYRUP: honey or maple/pancake syrup can be substituted.

ICING SUGAR: powdered or confectioner's sugar.

KILOJOULES: metric units used to express energy value of food; in the imperial system, the units of measurement are calories.

MACE: a spice similar in taste to nutmeg, made from the lacy outer covering of the nutmeg.

MIXED FRUIT: a mixture of raisins, sultanas, currants and cherries, with mixed crystallised citrus peel.

MIXED PEEL: a mixture of crystallised citrus peel.

MIXED SPICE: (not to be confused with allspice) a combination of spices including allspice, nutmeg and cinnamon, used for flavouring cakes and biscuits.

MUESLI: granola.

NAPPIES: napkins or diapers.

NUTMEG: a strongly aromatic spice. Use the powdered form or freshly grated whole nutmeg.

PACIFIER: something which calms a baby such as rubber ring, a dummy or a special 'friend' like a favourite blanket.

PARBOIL: to boil partially; half cook.

PASSIONFRUIT: fruit of passionflower vine, also known as granadilla.

PAWPAW: papaya.

PEARL BARLEY: barley ground into small round grains; often used in soups and casseroles.

PITTA BREAD: flat Lebanese bread, available in white or wholemeal, small or large, with or without pockets you can fill with delicious fillings; an ideal base for quick homemade pizza.

PITTED DATES: stones dates.

POACH: to cook in liquid just below boiling point.

PUMPKIN: member of the squash family, with a sweet orange flesh.

PURÉE: made by forcing cooked fruit or vegetables through a fine sieve.

RAISINS: dried, dark, sweet grapes.

RIND: zest.

ROLLED OATS: oat grains, heat-treated during a rolling process.

SAUTÉ: to pan-fry in butter or oil.

SOY SAUCE: salty sauce much used in Chinese and Japanese cooking, made from soya beans fermented in brine; many varieties are available, including light and dark, all tasting slightly different.

SPICES: the most commonly used spices are nutmeg, cinnamon, cloves, ginger, allspice, mixed spice and pepper. Store spices in an airtight container in a dark cupboard for no longer than 6 months.

SPRING ONIONS: scallions, shallots.

STEW: to cook by simmering or slow boiling.

STEAM: to cook by placing small cubes of food in a steamer inserted inside a steamer or saucepan of boiling water; an excellent way to cook food and retain vitamins.

STOCK: thin base broth for soups and sauces, made from simmered water, herbs, beef, chicken or fish.

SUGAR: Brown sugar: soft, brown sugar with molasses present.
Caster sugar: fine, white granulated sugar.
Crystal sugar: white, granulated sugar.
Raw sugar: natural, brown granulated sugar.
Icing sugar: confectioner's or powdered sugar.

SULTANAS: dried, seedless white grapes (seedless raisins).

SWEETENED CONDENSED MILK: milk which has 60% water removed, then is sweetened.

TIMBALE: a preparation of finely minced vegetables, fish or meat, cooked in a cup-shaped mould.

VANILLA ESSENCE: imitation vanilla essence may be used.

VEGEMITE, MARMITE: a vegetable extract used as a spread on sandwiches (registered trademarks).

YOGHURT: use plain or low-fat yoghurt.

ZUCCHINI: Courgette.

Equipment

BALLOON WHISK: a bunch of wire loops held together in a handle, for beating eggs, cream etc., until light and frothy.

CAN, CANNED: tin, tinned.

COFFEE SPOON: very small teaspoon, about 2.5 mL capacity.

GREASEPROOF PAPER: waxproof paper.

LAMINGTON TIN: oven tray 4 cm (1½ inches) deep. Grease and use as biscuit or cake tray.

PATTY CASES: paper cases or cups for making small cakes.

PLASTIC WRAP: cling film.

SANDWICH TIN: layer cake tin.

SHALLOW TIN: oven tray 4 cm deep. Grease and use as biscuit or cake tray.

TRAINING CUP: a small plastic cup, usually with a covered lid that has a small spout to drink from.

USEFUL INFORMATION

Recipes are all thoroughly tested, using
standard metric measuring cups and spoons.
All cup and spoon measurements are level.
We have used eggs with an average weight of 55 g each
in all recipes.

WEIGHTS & MEASURES

In these charts, metric measures and their imperial equivalents have been rounded out to the nearest figure that is easy to use. Different charts from different authorities vary slightly; the following are the measures we have used consistently throughout our recipes.

OVEN TEMPERATURE CHART

	°C	°F	Gas Mark
Very slow	120	250	½
Slow	150	300	1–2
Mod. slow	160	325	3
Moderate	180	350	4
Mod. hot	190	375	5–6
Hot	200	400	6–7
Very hot	230	450	8–9

LENGTHS

Metric	Imperial
5 mm	¼ in
1 cm	½ in
2 cm	¾ in
2.5 cm	1 in
5 cm	2 in
6 cm	2½ in
8 cm	3 in
10 cm	4 in
12 cm	5 in
15 cm	6 in
18 cm	7 in
20 cm	8 in
23 cm	9 in
25 cm	10 in
28 cm	11 in
30 cm	12 in
46 cm	18 in
50 cm	20 in
61 cm	24 in
77 cm	30 in

CUP & SPOON MEASURES

A basic metric cup set consists of 1 cup, ½ cup, ⅓ cup and ¼ cup sizes.

The basic spoon set comprises 1 tablespoon, 1 teaspoon, ½ teaspoon and ¼ teaspoon.

1 cup	250 mL/8 fl oz
½ cup	125 mL/4 fl oz
⅓ cup (4 tablespoons)	80 mL/2½ fl oz
¼ cup (3 tablespoons)	60 mL/2 fl oz
1 tablespoon	20 mL
1 teaspoon	5 mL
½ teaspoon	2.5 mL
¼ teaspoon	1.25 mL

LIQUIDS

Metric	Imperial
30 mL	1 fl oz
60 mL	2 fl oz
90 mL	3 fl oz
100 mL	3½ fl oz
125 mL	4 fl oz (½ cup)
155 mL	5 fl oz
170 mL	5½ fl oz (⅔ cup)
200 mL	6½ fl oz
220 mL	7 fl oz
250 mL	8 fl oz (1 cup)
280 mL	9 fl oz
300 mL	9½ fl oz
315 mL	10 fl oz
350 mL	11 fl oz
375 mL	12 fl oz
410 mL	13 fl oz
440 mL	14 fl oz
470 mL	15 fl oz
500 mL	16 fl oz (2 cups)
600 mL	1 pt (20 fl oz)
750 mL	1 pt 5 fl oz (3 cups)
1 litre (1000 mL)	1 pt 12 fl oz (4 cups)
1.5 litres	2 pt 8 fl oz (6 cups)

DRY MEASURES

Metric	Imperial
15 g	½ oz
30 g	1 oz
45 g	1½ oz
60 g	2 oz
75 g	2½ oz
90 g	3 oz
100 g	3½ oz
125 g	4 oz
155 g	5 oz
170 g	5½ oz
200 g	6½ oz
220 g	7 oz
250 g	8 oz
280 g	9 oz
300 g	9½ oz
350 g	11 oz
375 g	12 oz
400 g	12½ oz
425 g	13½ oz
455 g	14½ oz
470 g	15 oz
500 g	1 lb (16 oz)
750 g	1 lb 8 oz
1 kg (1000 g)	2 lb
1.5 kg	3 lb

Published by **Murdoch Books,** a division of
Murdoch Magazines Pty Ltd
213 Miller Street, North Sydney, NSW 2060

Author: Jacki Passmore
Art Direction and Design: Elaine Rushbrooke
Photography: Ray Joyce, Mike Hallson
Illustrations: Barbara Rodanska
Cover Calligraphy: Margrit Eisermann
Murdoch Books Food Editor: Jo Anne Calabria
Editors: Ingaret Ward and June Gordon
Finished Art: Ivy Hansen

Publisher: Anne Wilson
Publishing Manager: Mark Newman
Production Manager: Catie Ziller
Managing Editor: Sarah Murray
Marketing Manager: Mark Smith
National Sales Manager: Keith Watson

National Library of Australia
Cataloguing-in-Publication Data
Feeding Babies and Toddlers
Includes index.
ISBN 0 86411 169 X
1. Cookery (Baby foods). 2. Children — Nutrition.
641.5622

This edition published 1992
Printed by Toppan Printing Co. Ltd, Singapore.
Typeset by Post Typesetters, Qld.
© Murdoch Books 1990

Murdoch Books is a trademark of Murdoch Magazines Pty Ltd

Distributed in U.K. by Australian Consolidated Press (U.K.) Ltd
20 Galowhill Road, Brackmills, Northampton NN4 OEE
Enquiries — 0604 760456